Memories
of
Carlisle

True North Books Ltd
Elland
West Yorkshire
HX5 9AE

THE PUBLISHERS WOULD LIKE TO THANK THE FOLLOWING COMPANIES
FOR SUPPORTING THE PRODUCTION OF THIS BOOK

AUSTIN FRIARS SCHOOL

WB ANDERSON & SONS LIMITED

ARMSTRONG WATSON & CO - CHARTERED ACCOUNTANTS

CARLISLE COLLEGE

STEAD MCALPIN & COMPANY LIMITED

W VASEY & SONS (CARLISLE) LIMITED

First published in Great Britain by True North Books Limited
Units 3 - 5 Heathfield Industrial Park
Elland West Yorkshire
HX5 9AE
Tel. 01422 377977
© Copyright: True North Books Limited 1999

ISBN 1 900463 38 5

Text, design and origination by True North Books Limited, Elland, West Yorkshire
Printed and bound by The Amadeus Press Limited, Huddersfield, West Yorkshire

Introduction

Military and Civil Defence Exercises in 1952

D o you remember when....' is a phrase often heard today, and in response to the ever-increasing demand for local nostalgia we are pleased to be able to introduce Memories of Carlisle. In page after page of nostalgic images the book gives readers an entertaining glimpse back through the years at how people used to shop, work and play in the days that seem like only yesterday.

Many books of local history and nostalgic photographs already exist, of course, but the thing that sets Memories of Carlisle apart is the fact that it is packed with images taken from a period within living memory, chosen according to their ability to rekindle fond memories of how people used to shop, work and play in the area where they grew up. This is not a book about crinolines or bowler-hats! Local companies and organisations have allowed us to study their archives and include their history - and fascinating reading it makes.

We are pleased to be able to make it possible for them to share their achievements with a wider audience.

The book has far more to do with entertainment than serious study, but we hope you will agree it is none the worse for that. Modern image reproduction techniques have enabled us to present these pictures in a way rarely seen before, and we have attempted to set the book apart by means of lively design and generous and informative text.

It is hoped that the following pages will prompt readers' own memories of Carlisle from days gone by - and we are always delighted to hear from people who can add to the information contained in the captions so that we can enhance future editions of the book. Memories of Carlisle has been a pleasure to compile, we sincerely hope you enjoy reading it.

Happy memories!

Contents

Around the town centre

A very leisurely Market Place in 1933 with very little of the urgency of traffic, pedestrian and motor, which was to come after the second world war. Carlisle was to grow and, as its commercial life expanded, the number of cars and other motor vehicles increased. Here the young and not-so young enjoy a stroll or even a sit on the steps of the Cross. Others make their easy way to the Crown and Mitre Hotel. The motor omnibuses casually line up before making their eventual move. It is hard to imagine the hustle and bustle of the markets in the past or to envisage that different haste of future years. The Carlisle Cross or Market Cross or Carel Cross was erected in 1680s and its plaque explains the significance of it. The Dormant Book held by the lion in one of its paws contains the Mayor's oath and a copy of the city's bylaws. The city's stocks and pillory once stood on the Square and were later removed for safe-keeping to the Guildhall Museum. It is interesting to note as we look beyond the hotel to Castle Street and the Cathedral that there was once here a potato market at the end of the nineteenth century. Sometimes it is hard to recognise a town or city centre 60 years on after the changes it has undergone. You look for clues and eventually it falls into place. The significance of this photograph is that, despite the redevelopment, this is an instantly recognisable part of the city.

Above: A late 1930s look at English Street from the Town Hall and we can see the start of the development of the street as the place to shop. The trams have gone to be replaced by single and double deckers although the traffic and pace of life has yet to reach any more than leisurely. The stores and shops synonymous with the town are conspicuous here. It takes an effort to realise that at the end of the 19th century that apart from the market areas at this end of the street, English Street was more to do with private housing than with shops and businesses. Thurnams had been established in Carlisle as printers and booksellers since 1816.

It had also run a lending library and sold pianos but it is as a supplier of stationery and as printers that it was and, of course, still is, better known. The dome of the now Midland Bank formerly the Carlisle City and District Bank, is very prominent here. It had been Carlisle's first purpose built bank and once possessed a counter of polished wood and brass rails. Those were the days when banks had an air of sombre formality, rather like going to the doctors and often more painful.

Compare that to the openness and relative informality of modern financial institutions. But even today buildings like the Midland Bank do have an air of reassuring permanence and stability about them and enhance a city centre where the more modern may not.

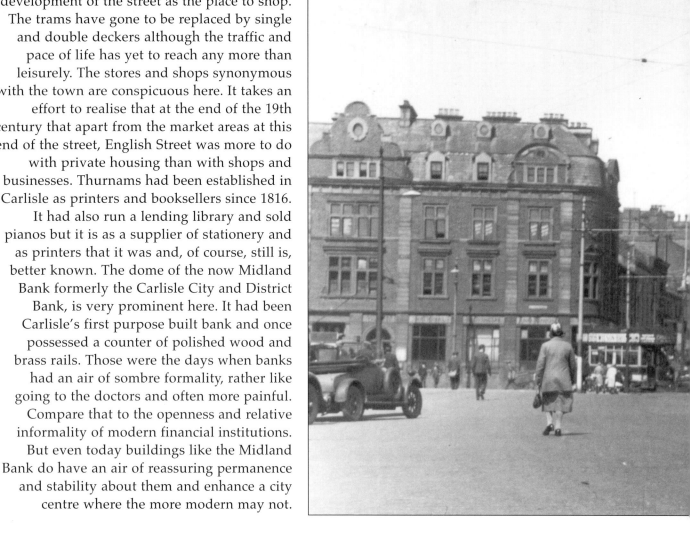

Below: A 1931 photograph of English Street showing one of the last trams, this one a single-decker, turning the Viaduct Corner. This was the final year for the tram as motor omnibuses were shortly to take over. Some very interesting shops and buildings are shown here and it is worthwhile comparing the scene of today. The traffic is quieter and there is no need for that lady or the gentleman further on to run the gauntlet of cars, vans, lorries and buses to cross the road or the policeman on point duty to be unduly stressed. At the corner of the Victoria Viaduct and English Street can be seen the Bush Hotel, now the NatWest Bank. It was opened in 1878 when the Viaduct was created by the demolition of part of English Street and Blackfriars Street, although there had been a Bush Hotel on that site since 1829. It had been a coaching inn and many distinguished visitors had stayed there, including Dr Johnson and James Boswell on their way north on the celebrated tour of the Highlands of Scotland. The hotel was also known as the Yellow House because of its association with the local Tory party. Even the post boys wore yellow jackets. At election times it was fairly certain that some of its windows would be smashed. English Street at this time was developing into the city's premier shopping street attracting locals and visitors who could have a choice of shop and purchase the quality of goods not available to them at home.

Below: By 1936 Burtons had moved to grander premises on the corner of the Viaduct and English Street next to the Woolworth building. The traditional frontage of the Burton building is very evident here. Burtons was known for the black speckled stone work on the front of its stores. This was stone imported from Norway and called, without too much regard for being geologically accurate, 'Burtonite'. Burtons also tended in its stores to put the upper floors to some use usually by having it as a Billiard Hall and Carlisle was no different. Just beyond Burtons on the Viaduct is the rear door to Woolworth's store and above is the Swiss Court Restaurant. Across the road is the Central Hotel and the canopy of the Viaduct Hotel. The sun blinds are out on the other shops here with at the corner of Blackfriars Street the well known grocers, Coopers, now Chapmans, and above are the offices of Carr's Flour Mills. Despite the grandeur of the buildings here, perhaps what does catch the eye are the two vehicles side by side, the hand pulled cart and the four door luxury Morris car, a sign of the times as Carlisle begins to enter a more prosperous age.

Above: English Street in the 1930s looking down to the Market Place with the entrances to the Viaduct and Devonshire Street easily made out. The tram tracks have gone and the street has the appearance of a very busy and prosperous area. At the Viaduct junction is the National and Provincial Bank standing guard on the site of the Bush Hotel. Marks and Spencer has developed its new store in what was Highmore House and Binns, now the House of Fraser, has taken over the Robinson Brothers store. Robinsons was probably the original pioneer of large scale shopping in Carlisle. A number of properties were purchased on English Street, thus enabling them to open their store in 1904. This new concept in Carlisle shopping extended from New Bank Lane to St Cuthberts Lane. Binns took over in 1933 and the gap that was the former Lane was evident above the first floor level of the store. At the corner of Devonshire Street stands what was the original Church of the Greyfriars with the Friars Tower clearly visible here. Later it became Carlisle's Public Subscription Library and Reading Room until 1891, but when the Library was transferred to Tullie House it was used for commercial business and underwent extensive alteration at the hands of Barclays Bank. They then demolished the building and on the site now is something more modern. The grand clock, which could not be missed by anyone in the street, belonged to Wheatley's Jewellers. Its founder was also the city's first fire chief, twice mayor of the city, and was responsible for the upkeep of all the city corporation clocks. Every town and city has been able to say there have been in its past people of some importance and stature whose sense of civic duty led them to use their wealth and influence for the common good. Wheatley appears to be one of those men.

Left: Any town has to have a civic heart. The town halls of some northern towns are grand imposing structures which seem to dominate the area and almost the town itself. Some have turned themselves into almost inaccessible islands; others by the scope of their architecture manage to retain that necessary stature. The grandness which is associated with these could not be ascribed to Carlisle's Town Hall pictured here in the 1930s. There is a simplicity and dignity about it which compares well with those so-called grand buildings elsewhere in the north of England. This building was erected in 1717 on part of the foundation of an earlier hall. There was originally only one flight of steps leading to it but the addition of a second certainly enhanced it. What the Carlisle Town Hall did was to be at the core of city life. The roads, the shops, the businesses and the markets all seemed to centre round the area and this was a natural gathering point for civic and public gatherings. Times change and the role of local government changed. Towns and cities were given more responsibilities as bureaucracy became a major industry. There was a need to centre the city's activities together so the Civic Centre was built. The old building however lost none of its dignity and still plays a pivotal role in local life.

Below: The decision to pedestrianise the area of street in front of the Town Hall looks in retrospect a good idea as it did open it up and allow the traditional civic centre to become a focal point of the city. Here it is obscured by buses and bus stands and they do detract from the view. The Guildhall, also known as the Redness Hall, to the bottom left of the photograph was originally the traditional meeting place for eight Trade Guilds, associations of tradesmen who decided on the standards of workmanship, fair wages, prices and the training of apprentices. Each guild had its own meeting room there. The Hall is now a museum of the life of Carlisle and was opened in 1978 by the Duchess of Gloucester. The statue in the foreground is that of James Steel, Carlisle's first newspaper owner. He edited the Carlisle Journal until 1851 and it continued to publish until 1968. His statue was moved to Bank Street after this area was pedestrianised. The tall building on the right of the photograph on Scotch Street belonged to a clothing shop with the grand title of the Persian Mantle Company. The street itself dropped into Rickergate and on the brow of the hill stood Scotch Gate, the last line of the city before Rickergate which was outside the old city walls. Nowadays you have to stand a while as you try to visualise how it would have looked then.

A view of the city centre in the 1960s, the flower beds surrounding the Cross, which while enhancing the area in terms of decoration, unfortunately proved, as traffic increased, to be more of a hindrance. This should be one of the great sights of Carlisle, looking beyond the Cross towards the Crown and Mitre Hotel into Castle Street and onto the Cathedral. The Cathedral was founded in 1122 and is one of England's smallest. It suffered badly after the Civil War siege and one interesting fact was that its bell wheels were removed after they had welcomed Bonnie Prince Charlie in 1745 and were not rehung until 1926. The present-day open aspect of the Cathedral compares much better than when the potato market used to be held there in front and high railings surrounded it. Beyond the Cathedral can be made out Tullie House, acquired for the city in 1890 to house the library and museum and also the School of Art was accommodated there. Today its asset to the town is in its Museum and Art Gallery, and a further extension is planned as a Millennium project. This whole area is symbolic of Carlisle's historic past and consequently - as the city develops - an integral part of its future.

Above: Tramlines and Telephone lines, both introduced to the street at about the same time, stand out on a very quiet Lowther Street in the 1920s. There is a quiet dignity about the street here which modern traffic does not allow for. The street contains many of Carlisle's finest old buildings like the one now housing the Royal Bank of Scotland and the old Post Office. But the building which Carlisle is really famous for stands imposingly at the head of Lowther Street where the south gates of the city once stood. The Citadel with its battlements and round towers seems to guard the city. It was built by Henry 8th as part of the city defences and has been very much part of Carlisle's history since then even when having more mundane roles as a Crown Court and housing some offices of the County Council. Coming down from the Citadel and the Court Building here is the Temperance Hotel and next to the tobacconists the entrance to the Lowther Arcade, still very much part of the area. In the background is the Crescent, private housing at the beginning of the century, but was soon to contain shops and businesses. At the corner of the Crescent and Botchergate is the Red Lion Hotel, then a great hotel but today not such an asset to the street or the city.

Right: This grand photograph was taken from the Cathedral, looking beyond the new Civic Centre and over to Rickerby Park and Eden Bridge House. In the foreground on Castle street is Bullough's Department store. The store is in the control of the third generation of the Bullough family and continues to maintain its reputation as *the* place to shop. Behind is Fisher Street. We get a good idea here of how imposing the Covered Market building was at that time and why it was another of Carlisle's famous landmarks. Work began on this market building in 1899 and Cowan Sheldon & Company made the roof, leaving their tradeplate on the main beams inside. The low extension on West Tower Street for the poultry market was added in the following year. The tower of the Fire Station stands above the end of the Police Station on Warwick Street. This is an interesting photograph as it shows Carlisle in the midst of some change, with a new Civic Centre, while awaiting further development at the Sands. What it does allow for now is for us to see some of the traditional buildings of the city to the full.

This is a fine view of Carlisle Cathedral taken in the early 1950s from the battlements of Carlisle Castle and it is one which the many visitors to the city over the years will be familiar with. It is interesting that often it does take a visitor to a town or a city, especially one with a great history, to appreciate what there is to admire about the place.

A lot is taken for granted as people go about their daily business. Sometimes a local will stop and realise this and suddenly say 'I never knew that' or 'Of course I remember now'. A superb photograph like this does make you think! In front of the Castle on Finkle Street, now a much busier thoroughfare, at its junction with Castle Street

now stands a hairdressers. It was once the artist's studio of Robertson and Gibb whose city portraits were a speciality. Above on Castle Street stands the white stonework of the Labour Exchange performing almost the same function today; only the name has been changed. This photo gives us a superb view of Tullie House and the buildings leading down to Annetwell Street, facing the Castle. Tullie House, at this time the city's library, is like many other buildings in Carlisle, a treasure house of history and appropriately is being extended as part of the millennium project. A photograph which will stir some memories, even if it is only of the old jam factory.

An original view taken in 1954 from the top of the Fire Station Tower of an historic part of Carlisle. In the foreground along Corporation Road is the Malt Shovel Inn, one of the city's oldest inns and where Robbie Burns once stayed. Beside it is the old John Peel Hut, well known to the members of the Women's Voluntary Service as a Canteen and Rest Room during the war. Hardwick Circus and the statue to JR Creighton, twice Mayor of Carlisle, is in the centre of the photograph. The construction of the inner ring road in 1970-1 meant that the monument had to be set at a lower level than seen here. The Civic Centre has yet to come and so we can have a good view of the fair on the Sands, the home of all the city's fairs, including the traditional Great Fair held each August. The old Cattle Market, with the last cattle sold here in 1955, is beside the fairground and in the background is the scene of the original Carlisle Racecourse and the appropriately named Turf Hotel. The main road across the Eden Bridge to the North and the East looks a very peaceful place here. There is not the traffic the road will endure in the next few years. This is a scene which will bring back many memories especially of the fairs held here, before the area around the Sands undergoes a complete face-lift.

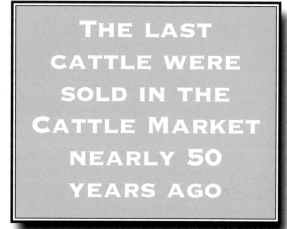

THE LAST CATTLE WERE SOLD IN THE CATTLE MARKET NEARLY 50 YEARS AGO

Denton Holme but was later moved to Silloth. 'Carrs of Carlisle' became a famous trademark and the large painted sign proclaiming this could be seen from the railway when approaching from the North. In the 1930s there was a vast illuminated one and by the 1960 it had become a neon one. Today the reputation for quality lives on under another name but the name Carrs is one which is synonymous with Carlisle.

Top: Porters was a typical example of how industries in Carlisle developed in the south and south west of the city in the early 19th Century. This was probably one of the oldest iron and brass foundries in Carlisle. It was a renowned producer of high quality grey iron and non-ferrous castings. During the 1950s, it was producing high quality casement windows. Porters grew up at the same time as Cowan Sheldon, Hudson Scotts (later to become MetalBox), Fergusons, Laings, Teasdales Confectionery and Carrs Biscuits. It is interesting that firms like Porters did flourish, because Carlisle owed nothing to mineral wealth, its main asset being its geographical position. Economists might say it is a more a distribution, transport and market centre, rather than an industrial hot house. It is its communications which have allowed it to grow, because road and rail transport have played a leading role in influencing the industrial structure of the city and its growth. Consequently, this industrial growth has brought employment and prosperity when it was needed and Porters played a main role in this.

Above: Port Road Railway Bridge dominates this view of this part of Carlisle as it divides Port Road from Calcotes Street. The bridge is now demolished. Lawsons, the joiners, are in the third generation of the family to run the business started by grandfather, carried on by the father of Jack and Tom. Under the bridge is the Jovial Sailor Inn, an interesting name for the pub considering how many sailors there would be in Carlisle, until it is remembered that the Carlisle Ship Canal which ran to Port Carlisle is just around the corner. Calcotes Street runs past Carrs Biscuits to Caldewgate. Biscuits have been made here since 1834, the firm having been founded by Jonathan Dodgson Carr. He built a school and houses for the workers in Kendal Street and Silloth Street thus following the pattern set by many factory and business owners in the nineteenth century. His corn mill was originally in

Below: A view of Globe Lane, where we can just about see Kelly's Ironmongers shop, reputed to sell anything anybody ever wanted. Globe Lane was part of plots of land which stretched from Scotch Street to the east walls of the city. As the city centre developed, so did the need for accommodation. Houses were built in these areas, together with warehouses and stables for the coaching inns on that street. In fact, many of the lanes were named after those inns. By 1930 these houses were considered unfit for human habitation and estates like Raffles were built to accommodate these families. That was one problem solved. All the Corporation had to do now was to solve the problem of what to do with the old properties. Unfortunately, that was not easily achieved and for about 20 years in the 1950s and 1960s, it was a time of planning and arguments. Like all compromises, the scheme of partial rebuilding submitted in 1954, satisfied no-one and by 1962 it was decided to completely redevelop the area. However, by late 1970 still nothing had happened and the result was a mess as many of the buildings had collapsed through neglect. Eventually a design was produced to retain as much of the character as possible on Scotch Street, while keeping most of the shops, the new much-needed library and the car park hidden from view. This had the advantage of retaining the old lanes' alignment. The result is an innovative pedestrianised shopping and business area which has its own character and atmosphere and is an asset to the city, even more so when the second part of development is completed.

Right: The nearly completed Carlisle Civic Centre brings Mrs Templeton and her mother to view. Whether they admired the new building is another matter. At least it was a good excuse to take her two daughters for a walk. The centre was described as functional on the outside and all the grander when you got in. It was certainly a product of the time and, of course, did arouse some controversy. People expressed their opinions at the time and still do. What the Centre did was to bring much of the city's local government departments under one roof at a time when that was considered important. The building of this centre, started in late 1961, involved firstly dealing with the problem of water as the site was so close to the River Eden and a pumping system was needed to enable excavation and construction to begin. The plaque to commemorate the visit the Queen never made in July 1958 but did a few months later was placed in the entrance to the reception area. If you compare this building with the old Town Hall, then 'functional ' is a good word to describe it. If it makes the running of the city more effective then it is good value for money. When in another generation or so this building has to be replaced by something more in keeping with the times, then the citizens of Carlisle may even look back on this Civic Centre with some nostalgia.

This is a familiar sight of the old Town Hall and down Scotch Street but taken from an unfamiliar position, perhaps from the roof of the offices of the Carlisle Journal. The Belle Vue bus is waiting outside Binns ready to begin its journey down Castle Street. On the opposite side of the road are the old offices of the 'Cumberland News' with one of its windows jutting out almost over the pavement. Next door are two well established Carlisle businesses, Thurnham's, stationers and printers, and Ridley's Chemist. As we look at this 1960s view we can see how effective the modern development of the Lanes Centre is. This view and one taken today would not look too much

SCOTCH STREET IN THE 1960S WAS A VIBRANT PART OF THE TOWN

different. The planners did an effective job there in enhancing a run down area whilst, as it is said in another context, 'keeping its shape'. Scotch Street here is a vibrant part of town as it leads to Rickergate Brow and behind on the horizon is Stanwix Parish Church. We just here see the beginnings of what would become a problem for the city. Where English Street meets Scotch Street and Castle Street in front of the Town Hall now has zebra crossings and the burden of the vast increase in traffic which every urban area had to face in the 1960s and beyond is beginning to show. How the city dealt with it is plain to see today. Other towns and cities were not so lucky.

At leisure

Below: It would appear from his pose that this young man was daring the photographer to snap him but when we think that it is 1937 he is probably just as fascinated by a camera as his friends were pleased by the paddling pool. The cost of this pool was from money left to Carlisle by the Heysham family to provide a small open space, Heysham Park in the Raffles Estate. This housing estate itself was created in 1925 and land was designated for recreational use. As well as the paddling pool the Heysham money was able to fund cricket and football pitches, a miniature golf course, ornamental gardens and a community hall. The hall was opened in August 1934 but in the past few years has been subject to the modern disease of vandalism and has been demolished. The provision of amenities on such an estate as Raffles in those years would have been quite an occasion, for this was not the age of plenty. This kind of provision was often due to private donation rather than from local government funds. Every town and city in the country would be indebted to a benefactor who saw the need for amenities such as parks, libraries and sporting facilities and wanted to ensure that the people would benefit. Looking at this photograph, the children of Raffles certainly appreciate this pool. Whether they were aware of how they came by it is another matter. Enjoy it while you can!

Above: Tin hatted soldiers spend their leisure time in May 1941 at the fair on the Sands and make their way up the steps of William Codona's Super Speedway Roundabout. Entertainment in those dark days was extremely limited and opportunities like this were to be treasured. The Football League system was abandoned at the outbreak of war and all players and staff had their contracts cancelled. However the government saw the benefit of having some kind of competitive football and the league was organised on a regional basis with clubs signing on players who were in the forces and stationed nearby. Carlisle United played in the Lancashire League. Cinemas were kept open but could not advertise as the manager did not know what film was to be shown until it arrived. The local Operatic Society abandoned plans to put on 'Wild Violets' and the Choral Society suspended all its activities, but the Musical Society carried on with conductor Charles Eastwood declaring that this was a time when a society such as this was needed. Petrol rationing curtailed many activities and even the local pigeon fanciers needed a permit to fly their pigeons. Like all other towns in the country Carlisle had braced itself for what was to come. A home guard unit was formed which manned pill boxes on approach roads to the city. Anti-aircraft guns were set up and a nightly fire-watch was established by a team of volunteers. Those and other organisations took up people's time where leisure pursuits had done in the past. The only trouble was - people's lives were at risk.

Below: A picture to stir some memories. This is the Senior Scout section of the 18th Carlisle Scout Group, the Wigton Road Methodists in 1960-1 *Back:* M Davis, A Walton, G Bryson, known as Gaffer, A Corbishley and a name unable to locate. *Front:* L Brown, G Kent, L Lightfoot (Senior Scout Master), A Mungall (Assistant Scout Master), S Horsefield - he obtained the Queen Scout Award and the Duke of Edinburgh Gold Award in the same year. Some of these young men obtained their Queen Scout Badge and travelled to Windsor for the St George's Day Parade, representing the county. The church granted permission and helped the scouts, parents and volunteer tradesmen to build their own scout hut and raise the money for the cost of equipping and maintaining it. The senior scouts took part in many activities like canoeing, even building their own canoes; climbing Great Gable on Armistice Day is one memorable experience, and of course camping. Camps were held in the Lake District, Fort William, Switzerland, Italy and Germany. The troop attended the Scout World Jamboree in Sutton Coldfield in the late 1950s and camped with scouts from all over the world. What an experience that must have been. They transported themselves to all their activities in a Bedford Transit van and even bought an old Post office truck. The 18th Carlisle group is continuing today to help to keep the Scout Fellowship and Scouting active in Cumbria maintaining the tradition and standards set by their predecessors hopefully with all the encouragement and support they deserve.

Customers of the Museum public house at Belle Vue gather with the driver outside prior to the annual bus trip to the Lake District in 1936. What part that young lad will have played in the trip is not known. On the left of the group is Councillor John Thomlinson, while the gentleman seated second left was pub regular Tommy Atkinson known as 'Akkie'. The gentleman seated second from the right was 'Tucker' Veevers whose local this was for many years. Over twenty years ago he would recall a very early landlord owning a greyhound which was raced in the Waterloo Cup. He could also recall that at the turn of the century there was Cumberland and Westmoreland style wrestling on the green outside the Museum when Belle Vue had its own sports. What the Museum was famous for was the large collection of stuffed animals and birds displayed, until recent refurbishment, on the walls in glass cases in what was the public bar. Whether the story that there was an eight-legged piglet as part of that collection is true is very doubtful. What is certain is the way the regulars have turned to fund raising for local charities in the past few years, so keeping up the tradition of this being a real local pub.

Above: *The library van here with driver/handyman, Peter Barratt, had proved a success and coupled with the upsurge in people's desire for greater access to knowledge and learning and for a wider range of fiction, the central library was at full stretch with staff hard-pressed. The congestion there meant long queues and, rather than wait, many would rather pay the overdue fine. The service was by 1967 in serious danger of being swamped thus not achieving what it was designed for. Something had to be done. Provide a second van? Extend the Central Library? The van was to visit more outlying sites but on a fortnightly rather than weekly basis. It would provide a lighter type of reading material for older people and mothers who could not make the journey to the city centre. But any would-be solution which papers over the cracks is no answer. However fine a building Tullie House was, and is, there was really no way it could provide a service and satisfy the public demand for more. Fortunately for the city in some ways, it did become a county responsibility in 1974. Now the range of services that libraries were expected to provide were beginning to go beyond fiction, reference and newspapers and the library had to respond to that. The redevelopment of the Lanes allowed for a new building. No more turmoil and frustration. What the city has now is a library to be proud of.*

Right: *The provision of a mobile library service under the direction of Miss Patricia Makin in June 1960 for the outlying districts of Carlisle was designed to ease the pressure on the central library in Tullie House. Here library assistant, R Wilson, can be seen in the library van's interior displaying a wide range of books. Another version of supply and demand seemed to come into force after the mobile library was introduced. The more books the library service supplied to the public, the greater the demand. The public wanted more. Thus the pressure on Tullie House just increased. The more people were shown the value of books, the more they were attracted to the relatively narrow range of books the mobile library provided. The wider range and scope that Tullie House could offer made the situation worse there. In other words the system was being rendered ineffective by means of its own success. More books were been issued now in one day than in one week in 1937. Hundreds of books could not be shelved and so were inaccessible. It was estimated that a quarter of the city's population had shown a desire to borrow books and the demand for reference books made the system made that area almost stifled.*

Above: Staff past and present of the Palace Cinema in Botchergate in March 1969 gather to say farewell to manageress Mrs Tyrell as the Cinema changes ownership and name and becomes the Studio Cinema. At the back of the group is John Wilson, still associated with local cinemas. On the far left is Jimmy Patton again long associated with cinemas before he opened a shop in Wigton Road. He was relief manager in local cinemas, including the well known Carnegie Cinema in Workington, as well as in the north-east. His wife Marge worked at the Stanley Hall cinema on Botchergate when Jimmy came to be relief manager/operator there and things never looked back for them after that first meeting. The Stanley Hall cinema had a reputation of serving the locals. A 'famous' incident in its history occurred when rationed chocolates were on sale at the interval at one performance just after the war. There was a near riot as the audience leapt out of and over their seats to buy these valuables. On another occasion the show had to be stopped when a pair of false teeth belonging to a member of the audience fell out of her pinafore pocket - it was a local cinema - and what a cheer went up when they were found after the loss was announced on a slide on screen. That is what made cinema going then very much different than today - audience participation!

Above right: Now a fitness centre, the Public Hall opened as a cinema in 1906 having previously served as a chapel before being converted to a public hall in 1900. In the early 1920s the hall was altered to give it an elevated appearance in keeping with other cinemas. Talkies meant the need to install sound in the early 1930s and this was the beginning of the great age of cinema going. Carlisle was no exception with ten cinemas in and around the city at one time trying to satisfy the demand. People's lives were to a large extent governed by what was watched at the cinema - almost the equivalent of modern soap operas. Audiences in the 1930s and after the war couldn't get enough of the cinema. It was part of the national culture, with half those attending being children and young people and, of the rest, three-quarters were women. So Gary Cooper, Tom Mix and Charlie Chaplin became household names and an eight year-old called Jackie Cooper, star of the 1932 film 'Soosy', was earning £500 per week. But whatever happened to him? We do know that the Public Hall continued to show films. ABC Cinemas owned it from 1937 and by 1943 matinees were held each day, often filling the 695 seats. The cinema maintained its popularity after the war, particularly among the young. Perhaps it was because it was cheaper than other cinemas. Perhaps it was the reputed comfort of its seats - especially the back row! But despite that, the competition was becoming too strong, especially as the larger cinemas could show Cinemascope, and to the disappointment of many a young heart, it ceased to show films in 1956.

Above: Surrounded by a well known local furniture shop the Picture House on Botchergate does not possess the presence some other cinemas had at the time and certainly not like those of today. The films were memorable and so were the stars of 'The Big Chase', made in 1955. Surely a blast from the past with Victor Mature, Richard Egan, Lee Marvin and Ernest Borgnine starring. Plenty to swoon about there. The female lead was Sylvia Sydney. Remember her? The great days of cinema-going preceded television and the other leisure activities which compete for the public's time and money today. Cinemas like the Picture House could guarantee a regular audience eager to be entertained. It had started life in 1915 as films burst on to the scene although it appears that on Sundays in those days it was used as a Wesleyan Chapel annexe. By 1922 it was advertised as cinema and cafe with prices ranging from

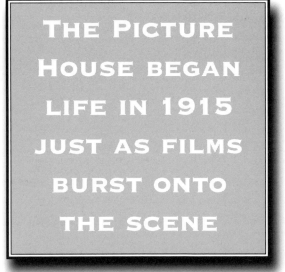

THE PICTURE HOUSE BEGAN LIFE IN 1915 JUST AS FILMS BURST ONTO THE SCENE

eight old pence to one shilling and sixpence. In 1929 it was given the most modern equipment possible to cope with the Talkies and could accommodate 1000 people. Ownership changed hands in the 1950s as large organisations sought to dominate the market and almost wiped out the independently managed establishments. By now it had become the Gaumont and prices rose as it competed with other cinemas to show the latest films. As people's leisure pursuits altered and the name Gaumont faded from view, it then became the Odeon with the same number of seats. Cinemascope, the successor to 3-D films and those activity marring glasses, was a feature but the tide was going out for many cinemas and the Odeon was one. The competition was too strong and in 1969 the owners Rank closed it. The hall was demolished. A landmark in the cinema history of the city had disappeared, leaving only the frontage as a reminder of its golden

A relatively modern view of English Street and especially of the Crown and Mitre Hotel. The shops around the hotel have changed hands since this photograph but that is inevitable. What has not changed for some years is the imposing frontage of the hotel. It is one of the oldest hotels in the city and was probably in existence long before 1745. Its original name was the Crown and Mitre Inn and Coffee House. The present frontage was built at the beginning of the present century when adjoining properties on Castle Street were demolished to make way for the rebuilding of the hotel at a cost

of £50,000 to how we see it here. As the city centre developed, the market areas were moved and the frontage was clearer, the true stature of the hotel came to the fore. Buildings of the past like the Crown and Mitre situated as it is today are of no use as monuments to that past; they must function in the present. Carlisle prides itself in combining its historical past with a modern image. The Crown and Mitre and buildings like the old Town Hall have a responsible part to play in maintaining that prosperity and the city's reputation as a most attractive place to visit and its citizens to live in.

Schooldays

The military precision of the Physical Training lesson for the boys of Bishop Goodwin School in 1924 may come as a surprise to those whose Physical Education lessons of later years were rather different to these. The word 'Training' as opposed to 'Education' seems to be appropriate here. It was a PT lesson. The free and active movement advocated as early as 1944 by the Ministry of Education compares with the almost military precision that these boys were taught by their teacher. Girls of course had a different type of activity placed on their lessons but often with a similar emphasis. The qualities the school was encouraged to develop in the boys, those of self-

control, decision making, self-respect, courage, good temper and a sense of well-being, are not very different to those a reasonable adult today would wish a child to possess.

The methods used were slightly different though. The opportunities for exercise and recreation were then limited and the PT and Games lessons were possibly the only occasions when many children would be able to take part in such activities. The breadth of events and facilities available today and the comparatively better health of the nation's young gives today's children greater scope. But why are so many children today overweight if that is the case?

Robert), Donald McFarlane (next to Harvey), Michael Campbell (2nd right), Malcolm Pickup (end of row). *Front:* Michael Patrickson, Michael Beattie, George Scott, not named. One or two gaps there but not for long hopefully. A marvellous reminder of what was a happy part of these children's lives.

Top: The children of Bishop Goodwin School in 1953 line up for their photograph and we have managed to find some of their names. No doubt hopefully it will stir some reader's memory and the list may be completed. One thing about these children, they do look well behaved as they stand and sit to attention. The names we do know are; Back: Robin Holliday (extreme left). Colin ? (4th left), Duncan ? (middle), Leslie Wood (5th right). Middle: Elizabeth Milburn (extreme left), Janice Jardine (next to Elizabeth), Florence Nicholson (next to Janice), Judith Hodkinson (6th left), Mavis Dunn (in front of Duncan), Joan ? (5th right), Joyce Baxter (4th right), Margery Heslop (3rd right), another Elizabeth (beside Margery). Front: Joyce ? (7th left), Pat (6th right), and a very smart Graham with possibly the surname North (3rd right).

Above: Belah School in the 1950s line up with their teacher - was it all one class? If so it must have been quite a task. *Back:* Alec Alves, not named, George Wood, Thomas Graham, Michael Storey, Richard Brough, John Carruthers, Brian Robertson, the hardworking Mr Colin Bell. *Second Row:* Dorothy Cutter, not named. Jacqueline Allan, two not named, Brenda English, Marion Errington, Sheila White, and the two girls at the end not named. *Middle row:* Joyce Abrams (4th left), Elizabeth Richardson (next to Joyce), Claire Bessey (4th right), Sandra Watt (2nd right). *Kneeling:* Robert Warwick (3rd left), Harvey Scott (next to

Events & occasions

> ## THE BORDER REGIMENT WERE STATIONED AT CARLISLE CASTLE

Crowds gather on the old Viaduct in about 1895 to see the parade of soldiers enter the city passing the Viaduct Temperance Hotel. Three theories have been put forward as to the nature of this parade, one being that it might have the departure of local men to the Boer War but there has been great doubt placed on this as they appear to be marching away from the railway station rather than towards it. The second is that it was a review of voluntary forces on the Swifts in that year and those from outlying towns had left the station by the Viaduct exit with the procession headed by the Pioneers walking in front with their usual picks and shovels. The most probable explanation is that the soldiers are regular troops of the Border Regiment, stationed at the Castle, entering the city. It has been suggested that they were at the final stage from Penrith of a six day march through Cumberland and the irregulars at the head are volunteers who were sent out to meet them on Upperby Road and escort them to the headquarters. Whatever, a large crowd had gathered to welcome the troops and they would only do that for the local regiment.

The people of the city gather in front of the Crown Court on Saturday 26th January 1901 to hear the Mayor, on behalf of the city, and the High Sheriff, for the county, read the proclamation that, upon the death of Queen Victoria, her son, Albert Edward, was to become King Edward 7th. The death of the much loved Queen was not unexpected for she had lain ill at Osborn Palace on the Isle of Wight for some time. Regular widely read bulletins had been issued regarding her condition. There had been some improvement in the previous week but then, as the Carlisle Journal's headline stated, there was 'continued anxiety'. In those days the newspaper had to be relied on by the public for information. News of

The Queen's death on the previous Monday reached the city the following evening by telegram. Immediately the city went into mourning. All public buildings flew the national flag at half-mast and there was a great feeling of sorrow. The Journal stated that the Queen was the greatest factor for peace the world had ever known. By the time for the proclamation of the country's new monarch there was some change of mood. The large crowd was ready to welcome its king with enthusiasm and the National Anthem was sung 'lustily'. Then the mayor met with a great crowd in the Albert Hall on Fisher Street to toast the new King's health. Carlisle had paid due respect to the dead Queen and to her successor.

HANDLE PARCELS CAREFULLY

The Christmas rush hits the GPO parcels office on Warwick Road in the late 1920s. It was the custom to hire temporary staff to sort letters cards and parcels at this time, a student's dream later of earning pocket money to work on the post at Christmas, either delivering the post or in the warmer surrounds of the sorting office. In 1863 Carlisle had its first purpose-built post office in Lowther Street and that was extended in 1900. The role and responsibilities of the Post Office widened when parcel post was introduced and telegraphs and telephones came under its umbrella, so new and larger premises were needed and the present Post Office on Warwick Road was completed in 1916. This is a fine building worthy of the status the Post Office held in a town or city and typical of the many fine premises which were built earlier in the 20th century. The present building, fortunately, still functions as intended. The Post Office has not succumbed to the idea of removing the main office to the back of some town centre store as has occurred in some other towns. The modern demands of having to be equipped with mechanised sorting and to accommodate the change to road transport for parcels did mean that these functions were removed to a new office in 1984.

Below: The headlines in the Carlisle Journal of Tuesday 6 January say it all. They read: 'The great storm and flood. Extensive inundations in Carlisle. Remarkable scenes in Caldewgate. Houses and works flooded. Serious damage and distress'. The fact that the Journal had a special pull-out supplement shows how extensive and serious the damage was. It produced a pictorial record of the great flood, not only in Carlisle, but also in Silloth. Caldewgate, a low-lying part of the city, was always likely to be first to flood and suffer most, and this photograph was taken in Church Street outside the Joiner's Arms. It is hoped that this beautiful car did not suffer any untoward damage. New drainage pipes were laid along Church Street and Bridge Street in October 1927 in the hope that the problem of flooding would be alleviated and everything seems to have gone well until 1968. Caldewgate was not the only part of town to suffer in this disaster. The area around Petteril Bridge on Warwick Road was badly affected and the football and rugby grounds in that area were flooded and damaged. The effect, not only of the flooding but also of storm damage, caused a great deal of hardship to the people who lived there. It meant emergency procedures had be taken for property repairs and the distribution of food. Fortunately, the city is now well-prepared for any emergencies, such as floods or storms, and modern engineering methods will ensure that the devastation caused in 1925 could never happen again.

Left: A decorated Castle Street in 1937 for the Coronation of George 6th on May 6th with as much relief as well as joy as the country tried to put behind it the memories of the three hundred and twenty-five day reign of his brother Edward 8th. In the previous year, their father George 5th, had died and Edward succeeded him only to abdicate and his younger brother to become King. It is hard to imagine today the turmoil and grief caused in this country and abroad by Edward's decision to give up the Crown rather than end his association with an American divorcee. Times have changed and similar events today might not have had the same repercussions. But then there was national distress. Edward's 'final and irrevocable decision' for the sake of the woman he said he loved has all the makings of a Hollywood movie except it was true and in those days it was vastly important to the country and the Empire. The father of the present Queen, a shy and retiring man, was suddenly thrust into the public limelight when probably he would rather have tended his garden and brought up his two daughters, Elizabeth and Margaret Rose quietly and without fuss with his wife Elizabeth, now Queen Mother. The affection shown to him and his family was due as much to loyalty as to a collective sigh of relief that the year when we had three kings was soon to be forgotten. The celebrations were long and heartfelt and Carlisle was as much a part of it all as any other town or city.

Above: If your dad was a Carlisle fireman and you were under 13 years old - no teenagers were allowed - then you could go to the Fire Station for the Christmas Party. You put on your best clothes like all the other children, and when you got to the party you were given a funny hat with elastic that went under the chin (and hurt a lot if someone decided to pull it and let go suddenly!). You played games like Pass the Parcel, Musical Chairs and sometimes even Postman's Knock, though that meant having to kiss the girls and some boys thought it was a soppy game. Then you would sit very still while Father Christmas came in with his big sack and gave presents to everyone. Once Father Christmas had to leave early and help the firemen fight a fire! When that happened, and all the firemen had to go to a fire, you had to sit very still - you were not allowed to move.

At the party, you could look all around the fire station, but a fireman stood next to the pole in case you fell down the hole. If you were lucky you got to dress up in a fireman's helmet (and found you couldn't see where you were going!). You weren't allowed

on the appliances, but you could look at the engine and even ring the bell. Mothers came to the party to help the firemen to get the tea ready; you got loads of pop and sandwiches and cakes, and at the end you were given a goody bag with a present and sweets in it. And what did the over 12s do? We didn't really care....

Below: The members of the Carlisle Fire Brigade march past the saluting base on English Street on Remembrance Sunday in 1953 on their way to the Castle. The line-up, as best as we can describe it, is: Leading the parade: Station Officer Harry Hale, Jim Robson, W Burbage, Joe Smith, Jim Templeton, Les Cowan, Brian Rogers, Donald Sutherland, George McPherson, Angus Steele, Raymond Carruthers, Bill Foster, Don Stephenson, Alan Routledge, Willie Allan, not named. The brigade was at that time well led, highly trained and skilful, dedicated to its work and more than once described as the best in the country. Here they show how proudly they can parade on this most poignant of days especially as many, if not all, of these men will have served in the armed forces before joining the service.

The Mayor's procession leaves the Town Hall and winds its way to the Cathedral. Heading it on this occasion is the City's Chief Constable, W Lakeman together with the mace bearer and the Mayor's Chaplain. On Mayor Routledge's right is the city's Town Clerk, Mr R Wilson, and on his left Alderman Mr Partridge, while Mrs Routledge, the Mayoress, accompanies him. The next group is headed by the Lord Lieutenant of the County of Cumberland, RC Chance. The interest shown by this ceremony and procession can be gathered from the size of the crowd. This ceremonial, very much in keeping with the traditions of the city, certainly attracted a large crowd of onlookers. Whether that interest in civic affairs has been maintained is doubtful. Local government certainly does not hold the fascination it used to. As government becomes more open and more accountable, then the mystique attached to it erodes. The role of Mayor, despite the qualities the holder of the office may possess, does not to many people signify the grandeur it did in the period here in the 1950s and certainly not as it did earlier in the century. But a procession is always worth seeing. The crowds that have flocked to see this parade will have been impressed by the sight of uniform and robes and the solemn dignity of it all.

Children from Ash Lea Street School sit patiently with their teacher waiting for the royal procession on Port Road, outside No3, the home of Mrs Templeton and her mother, Mrs Haigh, who are seated outside. Schoolchildren were out in force for the whole of the royal visit. A special pavement was reserved for all the children, as near to their respective schools as possible, strategically placed to get a good view of the royal car and procession. These children were an example of the well-behaved, but, whenever appropriate, wildly-cheering and flag-waving throng. Two children, eight-year old Pauline Fairish and seven-year old Michael Corry represented the schoolchildren of the city and presented a bouquet and button-hole to the Duke. The Boy Scouts' part in the historical procession was depicting the sacking of the City by the Danes, with Scoutmaster Peter Shaw of the St Aidan's Troop responsible for the production. Half Dena, a Danish raider, was seated in the prow of a Danish longboat, drawn by 'slaves'. Following behind the boat was a troop of Danes and prisoners, and a number of rearguard Danes were seen to be occupied with a number of bolder Britons skirmishing to rescue their fellows. Other scouts and cubs attended school in their uniform. They then went to Bitts Park where a site was allocated to them and 14000 children for the Duke to greet them from an open-topped Land Rover. A memorable day for the children of Carlisle who were encouraged to play their part in the city's great day.

Above: Crowds gather on Caldewgate to acclaim royal visitors to the city for the celebration in July 1958 of 800 years of civic independence. The Cumberland News headline the previous week read 'Carlisle was never more glittering' and stated that there would not be a street or avenue or road where the royal procession will pass without some form of decoration.

Carlisle was to be at its best in readiness for the visit of the Queen and the Duke of Edinburgh. English Street, being the centre of all celebrations was a particularly colourful scene, with white flagpoles bearing red, white and blue streamers and Union Jacks, with flower baskets suspended high above the street. What a week it was going to be, with special services in the Cathedral, an historical exhibition at Tullie House, the Border Regiment Beating the Retreat at the Castle all week, and of course, on the great day itself, a procession through the streets. For six months Carlisle had been preparing to give the Queen and the Duke of Edinburgh a glittering welcome to these celebrations. But at 9 o'clock on that morning of Tuesday, 8 July 1958, the people of Carlisle had learned that Her Majesty was not well enough to be present, and the first visit of a reigning monarch since 1917 would have to be postponed. The Duke of Edinburgh performed the royal duties alone and in such a manner that 'he triumphed over the city's disappointment.'

There were other great scenes from Carlisle's history in the procession. As well as the Scouts being Danes, another tableau depicted the visit of William 2nd, produced by the Boys' Brigade, while the Old Choristers Association were responsible for showing the founding of the See of Carlisle. The boys of Austin Friars School under the direction of Fr JB Hannon showed the excommunication of Robert the Bruce in 1207. Mr W Mulholland produced the capture and escape of Kinmont Willie in 1596 and the siege of the city in 1664/5 was the responsibility of the Townswomens Guild. The final episode appropriately, considering the long association with the city, was a pageant of the Border Regiment throughout the ages. The whole procession, with bands providing appropriate music for the various episodes, paraded twice; the first part was towards the Town Hall and then a rest at Caldew Bridge and then the second leg took in Dalston Road and the Newtown area and back over Caldew Bridge and again through the city. It was the most colourful spectacle ever witnessed in the city. Everyone agreed it was a triumph for those who took part and produced the tableaux and probably a bigger triumph for those who had to organise it. All in all a true 'pageant on wheels' worthy of the city of Carlisle.

Below: 'The procession that made history' was one description of how 1000 actors on foot, on horseback and on floats depicted the history of Carlisle. Fifteen tableaux so impressed the Duke of Edinburgh who was heard to remark to the city's mayor. Mr Irving Burrows, how thrilled he was to witness it. This glittering display had many highlights. The Duke saw Romans who marched Carlisle's streets so long ago, the saintly Cuthbert who came in the 7th century, portrayed by the vicar and church-wardens of the parish church of St Cuthberts, Rufus, builder of the Castle, Henry 2nd, the granter of the city's charter, presented by local NALGO members and Red Gables School. There was Mary Queen of Scots from the Girls County High School, Bonnie Prince Charlie and his surrender of the city in 1745 depicted by Stanwix British Legion Pipe Band. The recapture of the city from the Young Pretender in the same year was appropriately from the 11th Hussars, one of the units responsible over 200 years ago for that recapture. A more peaceful scene by the girls of Margaret Sewell and Creighton Schools with the 14th MU Drama group represented the city's fair during the early 19th century, just to show that Carlisle's history was not only bloodshed, turmoil and strife.

Bottom: There was nothing more satisfying for the large crowds lining English Street as the Duke's dignified walk in procession with the Mayor to the Cathedral. He smiled and waved to the large crowds as he passed, although this was not yet the age of the royal walkabout. But the crowds, disappointed at not seeing the Queen, soon warmed to the man as he tried to make up for her absence. At the door of the Cathedral he was met by the Dean and for the next fifteen minutes the Cathedral resounded to songs of praise and hymns. The Duke read the Lesson. This was another highlight of the events to celebrate the city's octo-centenary celebrations which had gone on since May. The Schools' Musical Festival concert was held in that month. There was a special exhibition covering all the educational activities in the city. There were band concerts at the Town Hall, a visit from the BBC Northern Orchestra and during this special celebration week the band of the 1st Battalion of the Border Regiment and Drums Beat the Retreat at the Castle. A memorable anniversary worthy of a royal visit and the many events to celebrate it.

Above: Carr's Biscuits workers on Port Road wait eagerly for the Duke of Edinburgh as he tours the city. This welcome was typical of what the Duke received. Many of the vast crowd had gathered as early as 7am in Court Square and all the way down English Street to welcome the Queen and the Duke of Edinburgh. But what a disappointment it had been to hear the Queen had gone on to London instead of alighting from the royal train with her husband. The Duke did compensate for her absence and the visit was described as a personal triumph for him as well as making up for the rarity of royal visits to the city. After a very busy schedule the Royal visit was soon over and by early afternoon he was on his way via Thursby and Wigton, where he received a tumultuous welcome, to Kirkbride to pilot his own aeroplane back to London. The question that everyone seemed to ask was when would Her Majesty come. There was an opportunity waiting as the Duke did not unveil the plaque at the Town Hall commemorating this visit. In fact it was not long before the Queen made her return visit. She came in October the same year. In view of the effort that the people of the city had put in for the July visit, that was what they really deserved.

Below: The official guests wait eagerly for the Duke of Edinburgh outside the Crown and Mitre Hotel where there was to be a Civic Luncheon. The Duke had completed a tour of the city and everywhere the streets were lined with hundreds of Carlisle citizens and the many visitors who wanted to be present for this great occasion. After the tour he visited Tullie House to look at the historical exhibition depicting not only the history of Carlisle but the industrial products of the day. Then he walked to the Cathedral for the service and afterwards to the hotel. After meeting with guests, lunch was taken in the ballroom. This part the Duke enjoyed thoroughly, talking to the Mayor about Trade Union matters, the Mayor being a local branch secretary. Gifts were presented to the Duke for the young Prince Charles and Princess Anne and for himself, though obviously intended for the Queen, a length of rose printed nylon chiffon woven and printed at Holme Head. He received a leather Ordnance Survey Map case embossed with the City Arms and made at Emcott Works. The crowds outside waited patiently during this two hour stay in the hotel before he left to meet the children in Bitts Park. Here he was given a rousing welcome both on the way there and when he arrived. This must have been a great sight, with those children in their thousands cheering their heads off at probably their first sight of a royal visitor. In today's world much of the Royal Family's life is played out before our eyes through television. In 1958 not as many as of those children had access to a set so the appearance of a real life member of the Royal Family so close was significant and memorable.

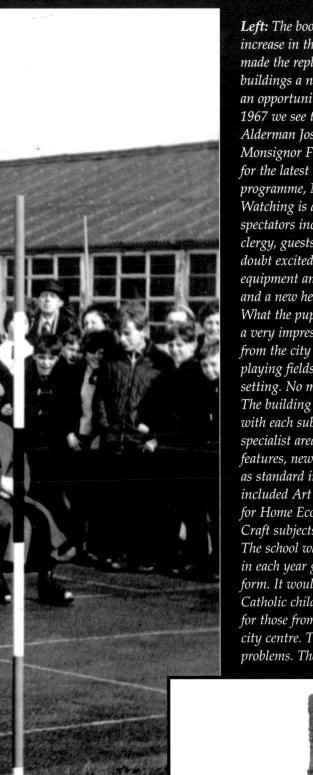

Left: *The boom in population and the increase in the country's prosperity made the replacement of old school buildings a necessity on one hand and an opportunity on the other. Here in 1967 we see the Mayor of Carlisle, Alderman Joseph Coogan, assisted by Monsignor FL Smith, cut the first sod for the latest in the school building programme, Newman School. Watching is an interested group of spectators including the Mayoress, clergy, guests and children who are no doubt excited by the thought of all that equipment and a modern airy school and a new headmaster in Mr Harvard. What the pupils were going to get was a very impressive new building not far from the city centre close to the city playing fields in an attractive open setting. No more than children deserve. The building would comprise 40 rooms with each subject having its own specialist area. There were to be special features, new at the time but regarded as standard in all schools since. These included Art Studios, modern facilities for Home Economics, Music, Science, Craft subjects and Physical Education. The school was planned for 120 pupils in each year group with a small 6th form. It would cater not only for Catholic children from the city but also for those from a 12 mile radius of the city centre. That would cause a few problems. The governors were antici-*

pating such a high demand for places that even before the first sod was cut, they had already asked the Education Committee to submit a project to the then Department of Education and Science to be included in a building programme for an extension!

Below: *Carlisle Castle provides a most suitable backdrop for the Regimental Band of the King's Own Border Regiment. The Castle was always regarded as the home of the Border Regiment from its formation and even after its merger and departure in 1959. The pageantry of the regimental band as we can see here has always been a stirring sight never more so than at the great parades and processions in the city. No-one can fail to be stirred by the music, the colour and the precision of a military band such as this.*
The three hundredth anniversary of the regiment in 1980 gave the opportunity to parade through the towns long associated with the regiment as it displayed its new colours. Like other military bands it took part in the Army's 'advertising' campaign called Keeping the Army in the Public Eye, known better as KAPE. The band, which always accompanied the 1st Battalion of the regiment, was disbanded in 1994 after another government review of the armed services. A great loss in many, many ways.

One-time members of the Border Regiment march proudly past their regiment's home, Carlisle Castle. It was in the 1950s that the regiment became after amalgamation the King's Own Royal Border Regiment. These men may well recall the colourful and impressive parades that it gave then in the towns of Cumberland as thousands turned out to pay respect to the regiment which husbands, fathers, brothers had joined throughout the years. At those farewell parades in 1958 marching behind the band of the first Battalion, they dressed in the various uniforms that the men had worn in wars since 1702.

Their tour took in Wigton, Maryport, Workington. Whitehaven and Cockermouth, where they were greeted by a survivor of the Boer War, Mr Billy Bowe, whose blue suit, bowler hat and cigar of Churchillian proportions made him the highlight of a memorable occasion. Other veterans of the two world wars and other campaigns shared the same sentiments. A great parade but sad that the regiment should lose its identity. Perhaps, as these men march through the city, they too will have recalled the Border Regiment's long and historical association with the towns and villages of the county. It was something to be proud of.

Sporting life

The Ash Lea School football team of 1959-60.
Unfortunately we have been unable to acquire the names of any of the team except that of teacher, Mr Albert Clulow, then a well known local sportsman. That is a pity for it is photographs like these which do bring back many memories. These were the days when schools football was very strong in the city and in the county with a great deal of talent among the boys. George McVitie was a product of the schools football. There were others then and in the future who had a lot to thank dedicated teachers like

SCHOOLS FOOTBALL IN THE 1960s SAW GREAT TALENT DISCOVERED AMONGST THE BOYS

Albert Clulow for. Other included Johnny Raine who for years managed the County Football team. Rivalry between schools was keen but relatively healthy and league and cup competitions had not yet began to be dominated by the big schools with a large number of boys from which to select. It was a good time for schools football, a time to remember old friends and opponents with a certain amount of affection and respect. It was also a time when for these boys school league tables only meant how well Ash Lea football team had done.

Top: In all Carlisle United's years of history the season of 1931-2 must go down as the time when the club was at its lowest ebb. Attendances had dropped to between two and three thousand and the club was virtually bankrupt. On the football side there was very little to shout home about with only 11 Third Division victories and a final league position of 18th. The FA Cup run was short-lived. A 3-1 victory over Yorkshire Amateurs led to second round home tie with Darlington but to add to the club's woes this was a defeat by 2-0. With half the season now gone, the board of directors announced that, because of the club's parlous financial position, it might have to resign from the league. Looking at the state of some football league clubs today nothing seems to have changed much. However, on this occasion at an emergency board meeting the directors all resigned and a new board was elected for a short period. Of course there were no simple solutions to the club's problems. Again shades of the future. Sell the assets ie. the players. Heelbeck to Wolves and McDonnell, top goalscorer, to Crewe, went in March. At the end of the season three more players left and even the manager, Billy Hampson left, although he did take over at mighty Leeds United. The only signing was Archie Gomm, a centre-half from Millwall. The clouds were somewhat lifted when Newcastle United played an end of season friendly at Brunton Park to raise much needed funds for the club. Not the best year in the life of Carlisle United.

Bottom: The 3rd Round of the FA Cup in January meant an away tie at the old style Ewood Park against Blackburn Rovers and a trip to East Lancashire for this happy and optimistic and extremely well-dressed group of supporters who appear determined to enjoy their day out. The team for this occasion is from left to right: *Back:* Tony Hill, Sam Cowan, Kenny Porter, next two not named, Brian Tickell, Alan Heap, not named, Harry Smith (end). *Second Row:* most not named,

Alan Reay (2nd from right), Ronnie Howe (next to Alan at end of row), *Next to Front:* Brian Reed, Edmund Vevers, not named, Ged Archibald, Gordon Wilson, some not named, John Lavery (3rd from right), David Wright (next to end of row) 'Dabber' Bell (end of row) *Kneeling front:* Brian McLeod, 'Bunny' Glover, Fred Handford, Eddie Kerr, Ronnie Walker, Charlie Hutchinson. Geoff Dixon and finally Jim Boyle. A superb win for Carlisle with two goals from Carlin and Wilson, repeating the League Cup victory there earlier in the season. Not such a short trip in the next round with the long journey to Suffolk and a 2-0 defeat at Ipswich. But all that is ahead of these supporters as they wait to take Blackburn by storm. Wonder what time they arrived home?

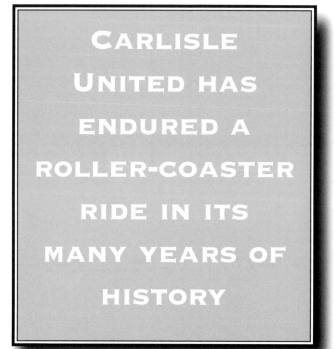

CARLISLE UNITED HAS ENDURED A ROLLER-COASTER RIDE IN ITS MANY YEARS OF HISTORY

Middle: A very nattily dressed Bob Kelly with his team at the start of the 1935-6 season: *Standing:* Parker (Trainer), Lloyd, James, Hill, Round, Harford, Manns, Webster, Henderson, Clarke (Secretary), Kelly. *Front:* Kerr, Williams, Landells, Shankly, Galloway, Cliffe, Johnston. This team of 1935-6 finished thirteenth in the Third Division North and if the away form had matched home form, the position would have been much higher. Only one away victory was secured all season at bottom club Southport while the club and supporters had only three defeats to suffer at Brunton Park. The FA Cup gave very little joy going out in the first round at Stockport by three clear goals. It is hard to imagine but the club had to endure serious crowd trouble; we think it is only a modern day curse. In the November match against Chester, after some decisions went against the home team, the crowd at the end invaded the pitch and surrounded the referee. As a result the club was ordered to close the ground for two weeks. One month later in a reserve North Eastern League game against West Stanley the referee stopped play and demanded a police escort. This time he had upset both sets of supporters and at the end he was given protection to leave the field unmolested. It had been a long hard season in many, many ways!

Above: The Carlisle United team line up for the first match of the 1951-2 season. *Back:* Wallbanks (trainer), Billingham, McIntosh, Twentyman, MacLaren, Caton, Stokoe. *Front:* Hogan, Turner, Jackson, Dick, Kelly. The opening of the season at Southport was like all beginnings one of optimism for the club and supporters. After all there had been some astute pre-season signings like George Dick from West Ham United, the tricky winger, Billy Hogan, from Manchester City. Manager Bill Shankly also had a new full back in McIntosh from neighbours Barrow and centre forward Billingham from Burnley. To say he was disappointed to lose this opening match at Southport by the only goal is probably an understatement. In fact he was more than aggrieved and said so. Things did get better and from September 30th until 17th March 1951, when a 4-1 defeat was suffered at Rochdale's Spotland, Carlisle was undefeated. But Rotherham won the league! In the cup Carlisle had its moment of glory. After defeating Barrow 2-1 and Southport 3-1 in the cup, the third round tie at Arsenal proved the magic of the Cup. Five thousand fans and a pack of fox hounds descended on Highbury. Hogan ran the Arsenal fullback, Lionel Smith, ragged and a well deserved no score draw meant an afternoon all-ticket replay at Brunton Park the following Thursday. This time Arsenal knew more than Carlisle and were relatively easy winners by 4 goals to 1.

Above right: The Carlisle United team which again faced Southport at Brunton Park 13th in the first round of the FA Cup on 21st November 1953 was lined up for the photographer thus: *Back:* McIntosh, Hill, MacLaren, Kinloch, Twentyman, Waters. *Front:* Rawes, Whitehouse, Ashman, Jackson, Bond. The result was not the one

Carlisle wanted and Southport came out winners by the single goal. The team itself finished 13th in the old Third Division North with 14 wins, 15 draws and 17 defeats. Alan Ashman again excelled himself with 30 goals for the season out of a total of 83. Ashman had joined the club from Nottingham Forest in October 1951 signed by the new Manager and successor to the great Bill Shankly, Fred Emery. Later that season came Jimmy Whitehouse from Rochdale. During his playing career with Carlisle Ashman made 207 appearances and scored 98 goals. He had two spells as manager, the first in the mid 1960s before he went to manage West Bromwich Albion and then he returned to steer the club to those heady days of First Division Football. He was not a bad cricketer as well at Carlisle and Edenhall! In this team there were some redoubtable defenders with the ever-reliable Jim MacLaren in goal and McIntosh continuing at full back, Paddy Waters, he of the short shorts, and Geoff Hill, one of the tallest players in the game at the time. And there was of course the class of Geoff Twentyman always shining through. Not a bad side that season but it did not achieve the results it was capable of.

Carlisle United at Shrewsbury on 3rd March 1951 during Carlisle's great undefeated series of games stretching back to the previous September and goalkeeper, Jim MacLaren, in full flight. It is said about Scott James MacLaren that he was not only one of the best goalkeepers in the club's history but also one the nicest fellows you could ever wish to meet. He certainly was a highly regarded keeper. He was the fans' choice in 1949 for that position in the greatest ever Carlisle United, team alongside such greatness as Ivor Broadis and Bill Shankly. He was born in Crieff a few years ago on 26th November 1921 and was signed from Chester in December 1948. During his years at Brunton Park he made 261 appearances and was renowned for his quiet calmness and authority. He was a member of the Carlisle team which took part in some historic cup encounters. In January 1950 Carlisle faced the might of Leeds United, including the legendary John Charles, in the third round and the more robust Yorkshire team were too strong for the neat football of Carlisle and ran out winners by 5 goals to 2, with Dick and Lindsay scoring. The following season the team went to Arsenal and more than held its own against a team full of internationals. Fine saves from Jim and a dogged team effort ensured a replay at Brunton Park. These were the years when goalkeepers had to be brave if not fearless The protection which today's goalkeepers receive was virtually non-existent. They were allowed to be shoulder charged and that was often the least of their worries. The fact that Jim MacLaren could hold his own for so many years in the Carlisle United team speaks for itself. It was always recognised by fellow players and supporters that Carlisle was a better team when Jim MacLaren played and that is tribute indeed.

On the home front

Above: The importance of Carlisle as a military centre was at its height during the first half of this century. The first world war brought with it an incredible amount of casualties. There was an urgent need to treat the wounded even if it was just to get them fit enough to return to fight in this 'war to end all wars'. Carlisle, because of its military presence, was a centre for the treatment and rehabilitation of the wounded men. This photograph shows a group of them with their nurses at Carlisle Bowling Green in September 1916 taking advantage of the late Summer sunshine. The soldiers were treated in local hospitals and also in larger houses which were requisitioned for their convalescence. Other wounded were sent further north and the city provided volunteers to attend the hospital trains as they passed through. Some of these men may well have been part of the large number of recruits to the Lonsdale Battalion of the Border Regiment. A large percentage of the 1152 were badly wounded at the Battle of the Somme. Within minutes of going over the top 25 officers and 500 men were out of action. At least these men look happy away from it all with pleasant company possibly to take their minds away from what has happened to them or what the immediate future has in store for them.

Right: The fact that there were so many Army camps in the area meant of course there was a huge concentration of the military at the outbreak of the second world war. The Army had built a basic training camp, Hadrian's Camp, and Bitts Park was used as an overspill from the Castle. There was another camp at Durranhill while the RAF had the large Maintenance Unit known as 14MU. Kingstown Aerodrome was also commandeered by the RAF. The threat to the city was great with the potential for a great number of casualties. As in the previous war nurses were needed and here in 1939 are some ready and waiting. They did not have to wait long. The evacuation of Dunkirk resulted in thousands of casualties and these nurses from Fusehill were soon given the opportunity to put into action whatever training they had received. It is doubtful if they could have anticipated the enormity of that tragedy in terms of wounded and injured and it was a significant pointer to the horror of war. It was all the more fortunate that the city and its surrounds did escape the German bombs but that did not deflect from the service these nurses gave when it was needed.

As in every other town and city in this country the threat of war at the end of the 1930s necessitated a strong call for civilian volunteers to provide support at home should that ever come about. Carlisle, again like many other northern towns, was indeed likely to be in danger from any bombing as it was a military, industrial and railway centre. The national response of the founding of the Women's Voluntary Service at this time soon led to the formation of a Carlisle branch. Then its members could at this local level prepare and train for the worst. By the time war was declared, the branch members, although having undergone training in such areas as first aid, home nursing and fire fighting, were probably unaware of the scale of support and activities they felt it necessary to undertake. A major effort was made to deal with the host of evacuees who needed homes in the area. The Citadel Station was a constant hive of activity as children and families and often troops needed feeding and shelter. The military often needed the WVS services after an air raid, or whenever 'exercises' took place, to provide food, if nothing else. Feeding stations, field kitchens and mobile canteens were considered vital and if the members did not know how to set about building a field kitchen using bricks and clay, they made sure they found out and 'pug' took on a whole new meaning when bricks and clay were the materials to build these outdoor cookers.

was a fitting way of describing the spirit of the members of the Carlisle branch. Mrs Semmence, Mrs Hunt, Mrs Timnkler, and Mrs Rae would have been proud to emphasise that as they represented the Carlisle branch on the decorated lorry in this parade. No wonder they are smiling!

Top: The first public parade of the Carlisle branch of the WVS took place in 1941 as the second world war had strengthened its grip on the lives of the civilians remaining at home. By this time the members had undertaken

Above: At the end of the second world war in 1945 there was a collective sigh of relief around the world that the horrors of the bombing and the resulting human suffering had now passed. The response was to give thanks for the end and also that this part of the world had remained relatively unscathed compared to other areas of the country. The Thanksgiving Parade which was held in every city, town and village was a public demonstration of the relief that it was all over, whilst also giving an opportunity for the country to express its appreciation to organisations such as the WVS for their work in the war effort. The members were not slow in reminding us of who they were and how they carried on during those dark days and 'Undaunted'

much work with members of the armed services, evacuees and refugees including many from the blitzed areas of this country. Carlisle had, fortunately, escaped much of the bombing but the threat was always there and organisations such as the WVS had to be ready respond. They had performed so many vital tasks in areas such as ARP firefighting, nursing, ambulance driving and first aid that their work was regarded as heroic as well as invaluable. On parade here are Mesdames Chance, Fraser, Honeyman, Dowell, Cavanagh, Sayer. Stokes, Ruddick, and Deacon whilst the crowd of onlookers on what could have been a wet day stand at the edge of the road, appreciative of the dedication to duty of the WVS members.

Military and Civil Defence Exercises brought out the WVS members' skills and ingenuity. Here at the 1952 cooking exercise working at the steaming pots on the ground outside Eden Youth Centre are Mrs Derdle, Mrs Fraser, Mrs Harper, Mrs Lodge, Mrs Davies, Mrs Fawkes and Mrs T Dowell. The members had learned early in the war to build emergency outdoor cookers with rubble from demolished houses and being taught by an army sergeant, an ex-chef in civilian life, stationed at Durranhill Camp how to build field kitchens using bricks and clay. A bit like making mud pies members recall. During the war that training had come in useful as four emergency feeding centres in local factories were staffed by members and they helped in the only British Restaurant to be opened in the city. After 1945 the emphasis was placed on Civil Defence as the country vowed that never again would it be so unprepared for war and not to be forgotten there were other new threats to our security bringing a danger of further catastrophe. Hence these exercises and the experience gained earlier certainly was more than useful to the ladies of the WVS.

Above: The WVS float here seems a more haphazard affair as Mrs Ruddick, Mrs Day Mrs Dinwiddie and Miss Ward enjoy the feeling that the war is over and they, their friends and colleagues can celebrate. As they wind their way in procession, they could recall the darker days of the past few years when their services were called upon and their skills were needed. They could remember in the early days of the war, helping to billet 5,000 women and children evacuated from Newcastle in one week in September 1939. They could remember acting as guides at the railway station, helping with ration books at the food office, making stacks of sandwiches, providing emergency billets for servicemen, bathing babies in the cloakroom basins in the Citadel station. helping to organise activities in Bitts Park for Carlisle's Stay-At-Home-Holiday-Week, making camouflage netting at Carr's biscuit works, promoting National Savings, organising salvage drives, collecting anything to assist the war effort from aluminium to pyjama cords and being interrogated in a most friendly manner regarding their activities by the then Duke of Kent. The ladies would no doubt wince when one of them was bound to ask 'Do you remember all that jam?' as they recall converting fruit supplied by the local authority into jam for the city's reserve stocks. These things and more would bring a smile and maybe a tear but on the float here it is time to celebrate and relax.

Below: Once a year from 1942 onwards the WVS office was used as a receiving depot for Rose Hips. It was known as Rose Hip Season! The hips were made into syrup as a vitamin C supplement for children. The WVS office was a receiving depot for the next 17 years as children and adult collectors bought their collections to the office. There members weighed, filled sacks with them and each week sent them to the manufacturers. In this photograph we see Mrs Mark Fraser and Miss M Ward and collectors with the 1947 crop.

The range of services widened as the demands for voluntary service grew. Fortunately the membership of the branch was often large enough to sustain activities, an example being that as many as 70 members could assist by acting as sellers when the local authority held a sale of surplus equipment in the Covered Market, The Home Help service was another area where the WVS was asked to help by the Medical Officer of Health and one of the branch members trained as a Home Helps Organiser. One service which the WVS did undertake and which was not widely known was to volunteer to go abroad to act as 'counsellors', though that title was not in use then, to male and female servicemen serving overseas,. About six Carlisle members undertook this task with, it is believed, one lady serving for nine years. As with all their activities and there were so many, the WVS approach was one of duty and dedication.

The open fire techniques were taxed during the 1952 Civil Defence Exercise and here at the site of the old Gas Works we see members of the welfare section cheerfully demonstrating how to do it. Miss Holden , Mrs Todd, Mrs Smith, Mrs Ross, Mrs Lawson, Mrs JD Hunter, Mrs Ashman and another Mrs Hunter cheerfully show their off their expertise. It is strange looking back at these photographs to comprehend during the war and afterwards how much the country relied on 'volunteers' to perform so many vital tasks during an emergency. During the war there were organisations like the Home Guard, the ARP wardens and of course the WVS to undertake so many vital basic tasks so that when the war was over and Civil Defence was a priority, it was assumed that the spirit of service was maintained. Certainly in the case of the WVS it was and these exercises took place with the members playing a vital role in ensuring that the paricipants were fed.

Above: The 'Meals on Wheels' scheme was another venture undertaken by the WRVS after the war. Now it began to extend its activities as the needs for its enthusiasm and dedication increased and this fine service commenced in 1948. From small beginning of serving 20 meals on two days each week, it was not long before they were serving on four days each week. The ingenuity of the members was really stretched as the scheme grew, in terms of acquiring the food, cooking it and of course transporting it to those who needed to be fed. The range of menu was widened - there is only so much soup that can be enjoyed - so cookers were bought and the menus became more varied. Transporting the meals was a real headache. Car boots in those days only carried so much and back seats were not very reliable - ask the lady who spilt sago pudding over hers! What was needed was a van and one was duly provided. This was heaven sent at a time when it was really needed. In fact this Ford van came by courtesy of the Canadian city of Toronto and its 'Evening Telegram' newspaper. This was a gesture of support and appreciation to this country which certainly allowed the WVS members to maintain and extend their activities. This followed on from the gifts of cases of chocolate powder that the Kinsmen Clubs of Canada had sent during the war, gestures of support so much appreciated.

Right: The Carlisle branch had always been proud of its Clothing Depot. It was always a hive of industry in the war as gifts of clothing from America and other friends of this country were distributed to evacuees and those in need of it. After the war, the depot was returned to local authority use and the depot became a back room in the WVS office in Scotch Street and later in the new office in Lowther Street. There was still a call for clothing from other voluntary organisations whenever there was an emergency in other parts of the world and this country.

The devastating floods in 1953 which bought havoc and hardship to many parts of the East coast of England, especially around Mablethorpe and Canvey Island in the Thames Estuary, bought a special plea for clothing for those whose homes and belongings were ruined. That included a special toy appeal for the children in those areas whose families were on the receiving end of the devastation. The response from the children of the city can be seen here as Gillian Beaty and her friend hand over their toys to WVS member, Mrs Lodge.

This little corner of the office became a centre for the collection and sorting of clothes as the people of Carlisle gave what they could in response to the public appeal for clothing for those who had suffered in the floods on the east coast in 1953.

Members, Mrs Wardle, Mrs Coulthard and Mrs Beaty, here are sifting through the piles of clothing ready for distribution. It is worth noting that Mrs Beaty, as Clothing Officer, was awarded the British Empire Medal in 1960. As well as the vast scale of the 1953 floods, there were the Lynmouth floods in the previous year. There was also a call for bedding and furniture as many people in these areas lost homes as well as possessions. The WVS in 1946 helped to clothe Austrian girls who had been brought over to work in Cumberland farms - a fact that seems strange to us these days. Not so out of the ordinary was a hurricane in the Caribbean which devastated Jamaica and brought a call for clothing for its victims to which the Carlisle members duly responded. It was not long after this in 1956 that there was a great influx of Hungarian refugees to this country and the public response to appeals for clothes was massive and once again the WVS was at the forefront.

THE WVS RESPONDED TO APPEALS FOR CLOTHES, BEDDING, FURNITURE - AND EVEN TOYS

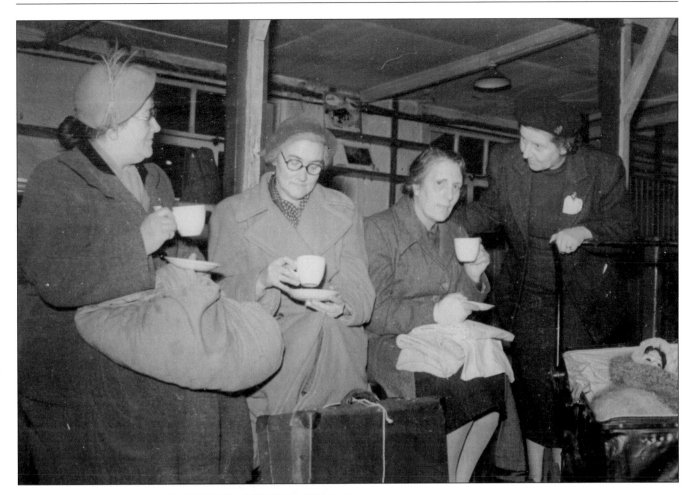

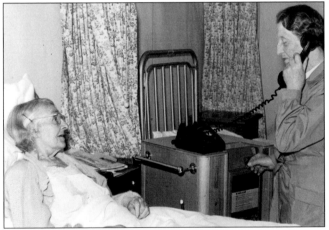

Above: After the war the WVS found that it was needed more than ever in terms of dealing with the many people, military and civilian, who needed help - particularly the many refugees from Eastern Europe who sought shelter in this country. The range of activities widened for the WVS as Civil Defence became a national concern and the hospital work which. had begun in the war, was continued. These activities included serving tea to out-patients, opening a cafeteria at the City General Hospital, knitting vests for babies, making cot blankets, operating the trolley shop, providing receptionists at the out patients department, a shopping service, giving concerts for patients, in fact anything to help the hard pressed nursing staff. The profits from the trolley shop helped to pay for telephone trolleys at the City General Hospital and the Cumberland Infirmary. On many occasions the value of this service proved to be inestimable and the efforts raising the money to acquire these trolleys were worthwhile when the real worth of the service was demonstrated. The trolley shop's profits were utilised to provide other facilities, including radio and television sets, electric razors, hair dryers and even bird tables. The activities of the WVS in the city's hospitals bought nothing but praise and gratitude from the staff, the patients and their families. thus making the efforts of the members so worthwhile.

Top: It was once remarked that this country's voluntary domestic efforts relied on the drinking of vast amounts of tea to sustain the activities people were forced to undertake. That was carried on during the 1952 exercise and here we see Mrs Coulthard, Mrs Shepherd, Mrs G Thompson and Mrs JD Hunter complete with pram in the Rest centre. This centre was known as the 'John Peel Hut' and was the last wartime canteen and rest room to remain open. It became later, after a period of standing empty, the local Civil Defence headquarters. Memories of that hut, the canteen on the Viaduct and the YMCA hostel also on the Viaduct would be about vast amounts of sandwiches, gallons of tea and coffee and the distress of people stranded by the war and seeking refuge in Carlisle. The post war exercises called again on the WVS to provide sustenance for the military and with typical endeavour and dedication laced with a great deal of good humour the job was done.

By 1951 the Carlisle branch had extended its work in local hospitals, having begun in the military hospital in Garlands in 1940. After the war, members served tea to out-patients n the Cumberland Infirmary, then it became a canteen and soon afterwards the trolley shop service was in operation in the Infirmary and in the City General Hospital. This was a great success all due to the devotion of the members. Patients appreciated it, not just for what they could buy, but for the friendship and kindness these visits bought with them. 'As good for you as the medicine, if not better' was one response. The familiar sight of the WVS members in their uniform wheeling the trolley from ward to ward did have a therapeutic value which cannot be measured - the only yardstick being how much the service was appreciated and how much patients looked forward to the ladies' smiling and friendly service. Whilst this was only part of the service the WVS undertook in the local hospitals - other useful work included helping patients in the out patients departments - the trolley service was certainly the most popular and it was not long before it was extended to the city's Eventide homes. Like many voluntary activities they are only appreciated when you are on the receiving end of them. Another important factor was the profits from the service, although not substantial by any means, did allow the branch to extend even further its work in the hospitals.

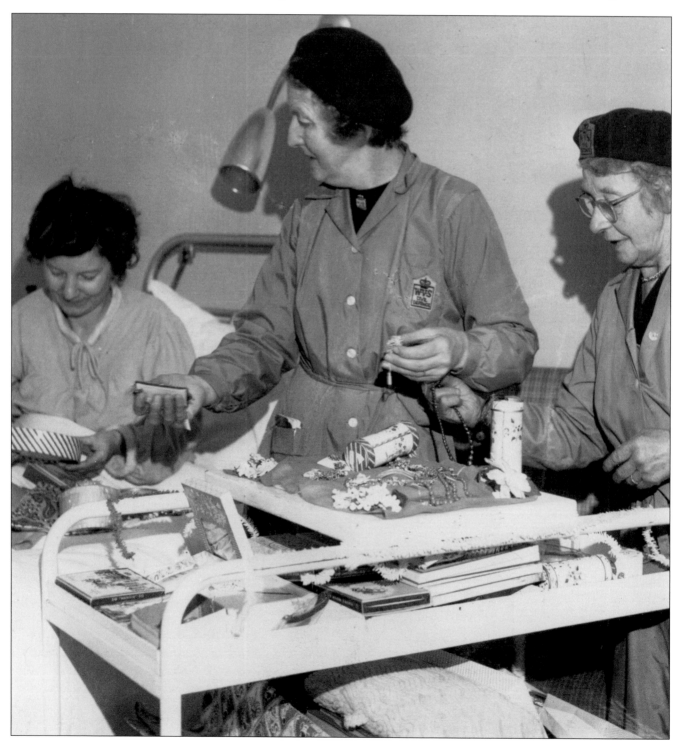

Shopping spree

Above: Marks and Spencers and Burtons as they were on English Street in 1930. We can assume hopefully that Montagu Burtons got its sums right when advertising its raincoat. The Tailor of Taste maintained the familiar frontage until it decided to change them in the 1960s. It was not long before Burtons moved as the need then to find larger premises was important in order to satisfy the demand for its clothes. In 1933 it moved to the Viaduct Corner on the old Gaol Site. Marks and Spencer built on the site of local tailors, John Redmayne, needed to extend as well. It went to the old Highmore House premises where it is today with the addition of another couple of extra departments, one being the old Littlewoods store. English Street has changed little and only in the shops that trade there. Like every other shopping street the uniqueness of the local businesses has given way, inevitably in a lot of cases, to shops that are to be found in every other town and city in the country. At least the style of the street remains. A visitor to Carlisle after many years away would recognise where he or she is and not search for direction. The changes that have taken place here have enhanced the street and allowed access for all.

Top: The end of Thomas Drinkall's shoe shop can be seen next to Clement's shop in this 1924 photograph of Castle Street. Thomas Drinkall established a shop on the street in 1843. Apparently, he had moved from Lancashire at that time, having learned his trade in a boot and shoe factory where he was foreman. He had moved here in 1901 after being on the other side of Clements shop. To the right of Drinkall's was the entrance to Brown's Lane where the Cumberland Building Society stands now. In this photograph Clements shop is displaying an 'Every thing must go' notice. The premises was the subject of compulsory purchase so that a street from Castle Street to Fisher Street could be constructed. This was to be called St Mary's Street as it was opposite the Cathedral and the gate to St Mary's Church. This new street was designed to link with the Covered Market's main entrance on Fisher Street and thus improve access to the market. The progressive development of the city had to involve change and that has to be accepted. How that change is brought about will always cause some controversy. This change was no exception nor will it be the last time there is a debate during this or any other city's development.

The warmth of a sunny Carlisle day in 1899 brings out the ladies' parasols as they do their shopping in the Green Market. This is where vegetables were sold and the L-shaped market had Guildhall on its left and the Town Hall on its right. The Green market was the only street in Carlisle to retain its market name. Market days were on Wednesday and Saturday and during August there was a continuous market for fifteen days at the Great Fair. A shorter time was spent on the selling of grain on English Street; it was reckoned all business was conducted in one hour. The Sands was the venue of the cattle market and hay and pigs were sold on Bitts Park. It is interesting today that the term 'Paddy's Market' on Caldewgate is in use, for that was the Irish quarter of the city at the end of the last century. The markets at this time had all undergone a tremendous reorganisation resulting in an improvement in conditions for everyone and the picture of the shoppers here in front of Watt's grocers shop on Glovers Row gives the impression that all is a very pleasant experience. That is before the trams came and caused disruption, forcing Watts to move to Bank Street where it still retains a prominent position for discerning tea and coffee drinkers.

Left: One boy and his dog stand guard outside the corner shop at 80A Charles Street. This is a typical example of shops serving the local community up until the mid-1970s when this photograph was taken. But people's shopping habits had begun to change. They wanted choice and diversity. They became more discriminating as the emphasis was on the consumer satisfaction replacing the 'take it or leave it' attitude once adopted by some establishments. The struggle of small family-owned shops such as this to compete with multi-national chain stores has been a long one and the battle for custom did not stop there. A shop like Maypole, which was once regarded as one of the more economical stores at which to shop, also found life difficult as the competition became fierce. With, amongst others, Lipton, Home and Colonial and Broughs it became part of the Home and Colonial Group but even then eventually foundered. The struggle of town centre shops to cope with the competition of edge of town shopping centres is a common one in this country and certainly applies to Carlisle. Yet, many of these small corner shops have survived for the obvious reasons of convenience and service. They are an asset to the community they serve but there have been many casualties. The consumer is now king in many many ways.

Above: Fisher Street, pictured here in 1958, has the appearance of a thriving commercial thoroughfare. There have been changes to it since and the vitality which we see here may not be as evident today. One of Carlisle's oldest inns, the King's Head, is just off to the left of this photograph and the plaque sited on the wall outside tells us this and more. The other inns about the same vintage are the Woolpack on Milburn Street and the Sportsman behind the old Binns. Rosemary Lane, leading to Scotch Street, is to the left of the King's Head as we look to the Town Hall and the other well known shops on this side of the street were Huthart's drapers and Telford's Radio. Is that a Silver Cross pram being so admired? Mr A Jenkins is deep in conversation outside his grocery and provisions shop while next door is his brother's butchers selling very good quality meat then. Still connected with meat, the name Pioneer lives on today, though not in Fisher Street. In terms of pedestrian traffic, Fisher Street is not so busy today as it is here, where it buzzes with life and vitality. With it being so narrow there was an added sense of urgency as it played a significant part in the commercial life of the city. But times change and the intimacy which is evident here has probably moved to places like the Lanes.

Below: A fruit and flower stall in Carlisle Covered Market belonging to the McBride family. On the left here in 1952 is Mrs Jean McBride who started the business in 1890 and to her left is her daughter, Jinny. Family businesses like the McBrides are usually the mainstays of markets and build up a reputation and following which lasts for generations as the family carries it on. Even today the McBride family supply fruit and veg with the same good humour. Carlisle Covered Market was the attraction in the city and locals and visitors alike flocked to it. Two Canadians, whenever they made their frequent visits to Carlisle, always made the market their first port of call. The market was the venue for shows and meetings and exhibitions and remained virtually unchanged until a major refurbishment in the 1990s. These changes have been controversial but so is any change of long standing buildings and traditions. They always have and it will be forever thus. What the McBrides and others did was to help to create a market which was unique to Carlisle; present day market members have the duty to ensure that the atmosphere and tradition is not lost and the area does not become another shopping mall. Malls are easy to create; the distinctiveness of the covered market is hard to replace.

Right: Two businesses on Warwick Road in 1951 which should give a reminder of a different world. In the doorway of the offices of the 'Newcastle Journal', is Billy White selling newspapers. Advertised in the windows are the names of newspapers which earn the title 'Memories are made of these', a roll call of those soon forgotten; the Sunday papers like The Graphic, Empire News, Sun, Chronicle and the Daily Graphic. There is only the Sunday Times still bearing at least the same name. Times do change in the newspaper industry, even locally. In Carlisle over the years there has been the Examiner, the Advertiser, the Echo, the Express, the Chronicle and the Journal. More recently the Carlisle based Cumbrian Newspapers followed the national trend of collecting titles by acquiring newspapers which serve the areas around West Cumberland and Furness as well as those serving the Carlisle area. Next door to the Journal is ET Roberts selling 78inch records on the HMV and Decca labels. This is the age when pop music 'took off'. Think of those early days of scouring the Musical Express every Friday for news of the top twenty. There is also a search on for the 'Shooting Stars of 1952', a pop talent contest presumably and those who thought that line dancing was a modern invention should look at the other poster in the window. Who says nothing ever happened before the nineties?

Annetwell Street, facing the Castle, was part of a crescent built to improve the approach along Devonshire Walk to the Royal Show and, until the area was developed in the 1960s, was a main transport thoroughfare.

Apart from being a haven for the discerning sweet toothed customer with a selection of Callard and Bowser's and Needler's finest products - think of Humbugs, Black Bullets, Barley Sugars, Lemon Drops, Pear Drops and Honey Toffees, Butterscotch, Mint Balls, Sherbet Dabs - Mrs Lawley's shop on

IN THE EARLY 1980s A DUMPER TRUCK FELL DOWN THE WELL THAT EVERYONE SAID WAS NOT THERE

Annetwell Street, which is today taken over by the builders and developers, was the centre of some controversy. For years she kept telling anyone who cared to listen that Annetwell Street did not have that name for nothing. She always insisted there was a well underneath her shop and that was why the street was so named. Her story was doubted. The sceptics were proved wrong. Mrs Lawley was right. When developers began to build on the street in the early 1980s, a builder's dumper truck fell down it. A case of 'I told you so!' And the well is still there!

On the move

Above: Travel by rail at the beginning of this century was a great experience and stations like the Carlisle Citadel took on an appearance of the grandeur of a stately home. Station Masters wore top hats and frock coats, officials wore bowlers and dark suits and there was always the air of the great occasion. Here we are in the hey day of Carlisle passenger traffic and a group of railway officials plus a lad carrying what looks like a picnic hamper stand in stately pose beside the London and North Western Railway Locomotive, Resplendent Experiment 'City of Glasgow' number 1669, as it awaits its departure. The demand for rail travel in these Edwardian times was such that during a five hour period between 1 am and 6 am in 1906, twenty passenger trains stopped at the Citadel Station going North. This was also the time when competition between railway companies was fierce, particularly between those serving the East Coast line and those serving the West. The race to Scotland was on and lasted for many years. Speed was of the essence. Journey times were methodically recorded and if minutes were gained then that achievement would be widely proclaimed. What was realised was the importance of Carlisle as a railway centre and the LNWR, whilst claiming to be the country's premier line, recognised this and paid Carlisle the compliment of naming two of its locomotives 'City of Carlisle'.

Below: Four 4-4-2 tank engines languishing in a siding at Durranhill before the dreadful fate of being sent to be cut up. The engines originally belonged to the London, Tilbury and Southend lines and were at one time sent from Essex in the 1950s to Dundee Tay Bridge as replacements for the C15s and C16s. There they were not regarded as suitable and, as one report stated, they received 'a frosty welcome'. They were sent back but only reached Carlisle and here they await their fate. It is interesting that Carlisle being such a railway centre should in the past few years have developed its own rail trail, another form of heritage trail, especially as a lot of what was part of its rail history could have been in danger of being soon long forgotten. The locomotive sheds as at Upperby, the buildings like the grand Citadel Station, the bridges such as the Nelson Bridge, the goods yards, the depots, the old lines and other properties are part of this history. All that is worth preserving not only in written and photographic record but also as a real life experience. After all, it was not for nothing that Carlisle was, and for many still is, a centre for railway enthusiasts and for that fact only, the past is worth preserving.

Above: The grand sight of the 'Royal Scot', here passing no.3 signal box after leaving Carlisle on its way to Glasgow. The decision in 1968 by British Rail to do away with steam could have meant that the sight of a steam locomotive hauling a train was gone for ever. British Rail had also decreed that no preserved steam locomotive would ever be allowed to run on its lines again. What that organisation had not realised was that to many people the magic of steam is indefinable and a steam locomotive is almost a living thing. It was not just schoolboys in short trousers standing on the Citadel Station collecting engine numbers before other interests dominated their (our) lives but what one steam fan called 'an incurable disease'. The powers of British Rail did not reckon with the enthusiasm and determination of Steam Preservation Societies and three years later one steam locomotive, 'King George V', undertook an 8-day exhibition tour of the country and thousands flocked to see it. The rest they say is history. British Rail could not ignore it. The movement had begun and has not stopped growing. The same enthusiast sums it up thus: 'There is nothing to match the awesome power of an express locomotive hauling a heavy train at main line speeds'. It does not need a second glance at this photograph to understand and appreciate this.

Right: A 1890s bird's eye view of in the distance the imposing Cathedral and the churches of St Cuthbert's and St Mary's, and closer, of English Damside below West Walls with the railway heading north over the arches which later were turned into shops. This was the time of the great railway age and by this time there were seven railways operating into Carlisle. They bisected Carlisle from the north west to the south east and with such passenger and goods traffic necessitating the provision of marshalling yards, it ensured that there were opportunities for the population to get jobs. Not only did the railways expand, so did the roads with Eden Bridge forming a very busy link between England and Scotland. New industries came to the city and existing ones expanded. In this photograph can be seen Errington's Leather works, what was Ferguson's Cotton factory and the whitewashed building of Pattison's Brewery. The city grew not only in terms of transport, population and industry but also in terms of stature. That was as long as people did not regard it as a staging post on the main north-south highway but as a place worthy of the name City. It must be annoying when Carlisle is referred to as the 'Gateway to Scotland'. It is much more significant than that.

Left: One of the last 'clippies' to work on the Carlisle bus service sits on the steps of the Cross in the early 1950s shortly before the conductor service was done away with and drivers were having to do all the work. It is thought this lady's name was Mrs Smith. Carlisle was one of the few places which did not run a municipal bus service and that left Ribble, Caledonian, known better as SMT, United and Cumberland Motor Services to vie for custom. CMS, under the direction of the Magean family - local cricketers will recognise that name - was the largest of the four companies to operate in the county. The history of Carlisle's public transport is of trams, before they were removed from service in 1931, competing with motor buses. This was made even more confusing as there were so many bus operators in the city - by 1926 there were 30. The trams could not compete. They were notoriously slow and of course restricted in their routes. The situation was made worse for them as the city was expanding outwards beyond the tramlines. It was at this time the Corporation tried a buy-out of the system but was not successful. Ribble bought the trams and in 1931 they were withdrawn from the streets with all the privately owned buses taken over by the above four operators. In hindsight it may have been in the city's best interest in those days to have had a corporation or even a joint county council and city owned service, although whether the economics of

it would have made it a viable undertaking is for others to answer. But the system by and large remains today as it was then.

Above: The age of the car is upon us as we look at the cobbled surface of English Street in the 1960s at its junction with the Viaduct. Quite a change is beginning to take place. The car population is increasing rapidly although parking is still free. Businesses are thriving, hence the rise in the number of lorries and vans and the styles of motor car are more varied. The leisured pace of pre-war years is giving way to the 'busy-ness' of the more recent times. The uniqueness of the street in terms of the number of small independent traders or businesses is beginning to fade owing to the distinct revolution in consumer spending and its associated increase in the number of shops willing to accommodate this phenomenon. Small family-type businesses started to struggle and the influx of national shops and stores began to dominate main shopping areas. Shops and stores like Marks and Spencer, Woolworths, Boots and WH Smith could at one time live side by side with these local businesses. But many of the latter were now forced to change their character, to move or even to close. Town and city centres began to lose that uniqueness and looked like any other. Planners took some time to realise this. At least Carlisle has not suffered in the way others have. It still looks like Carlisle.

At work

Above: Autumn in 1958 in Carlisle means gathering the fallen leaves in Victoria Park now part of Bitts Park. Being so close to the city centre made this a favourite place for recreation for the people of Carlisle. Carlisle's parks, all close to the River Eden, provided 169 acres of space all within a quarter of a mile of the city centre. Bitts Park with the recent work completed on the landscaping is the park which has undergone the greatest changes but the work there has bought its own reward . Rickerby Park is the more modern and was opened in 1932 in memory of the men who died in the first world war. Victoria Park, with the monument to Queen Victoria in the centre, was opened in 1902 and has remained virtually unchanged. It is a tribute to the foresight of the planners whose idea it was to create such an amenity for the people of the city. Those Victorians who were responsible for the design of many of our towns and cities are to be remembered for the wisdom that provided such places for recreation close to the centre. The parks and other amenities which are their legacy enhanced the quality of the town itself and of the lives of people who lived and worked there. They continue to do so and we lose them at our peril.

Right: A dirty and hazardous process of the re-laying of Castle Street in 1930 and that applies to the workmen and the locals alike. The tar certainly had its own distinctive smell, but all that smoke was far from pleasant. These were the days before Health and Safety at work became a real issue. The little girl on the edge of the pavement would not be allowed so close today and the ubiquitous traffic lights and cones and red tape are nowhere to be seen. The street itself with the nearby grandeur of the Castle and the equally grand buildings certainly was, and is, a Carlisle 'treasure.' Changes it has undergone but generally the style and the view has changed little. There is still Tullie House - a great asset to the city - and the shops and offices leading up to the Cathedral. But as we approach the end of the twentieth century the character of the area will change to commemorate the beginning of the twenty-first.

The Street and its surrounds will take on an extra aspect. So, as these workmen transformed the character of the street in the 1930s to accommodate progress in transport, so the city looks forward in the same way not this time to change but to enhance.

Above: The fleet of vehicles of the Carlisle Steam Laundry with their drivers in their ultra smart uniforms and caps almost chauffeur-like are paraded for the camera in the late 1940s. By this time the laundry had been on the go in Warwick Road since the end of the nineteenth century and obviously from this photograph had flourished. In those early days its full name was the Carlisle Steam Laundry and Carpet Beating Company and as it grew then the premises were extended. Its chimney, like Dixons, became a Carlisle landmark particularly as the laundry was sited in the flatlands adjacent to the river. The 1940s would be the age when the laundry was in its heyday. Very few of the gadgets we take for granted in our homes today were available then and if they were, not many families could afford them. At this time the laundry itself was not well equipped and most if not all of the washing and ironing was done by hand (and female hands at that) while male employees wore the smart uniforms and drove the vans in style. Time will change many things, we are led to believe.

Right: The Carlisle Steam Laundry was well aware of the power of friendly persuasion in its advertising, looking at the side of its stall here at the row of children's clothes. ' Next time I finks I'll send it with mummy's to the Carlisle Steam Laundry.' The Laundry also would remind the public in its advertising blurb of the importance of a laundry being above suspicion in its Sanitary and Hygienic Appointments; it should be in a clean and open situation; it should have a pure and limitless water-supply so that the washing and rinsing may be pure; it should have open-air drying grounds, free from smoke and dust, and its prime statement was to the effect that it was impossible to over-estimate the importance of the Laundry in domestic economy. It did appear that the Carlisle laundry had the confidence of the local public and its competition was not too strong. The others at one time were the Lakeland Laundry on London Road and the House of Providence at Durran Hill. Soon the golden age of the consumer will be upon us and as Harold McMillan will tell us 'You've never had it so good'. More and more families will do their own laundry but until then keep an eye on Carlisle Steam Laundry's special offers!

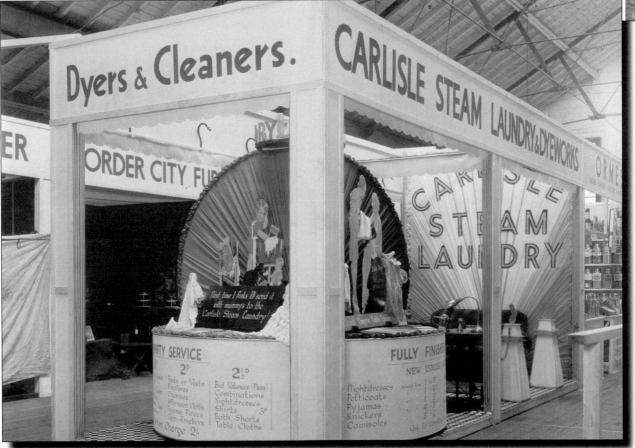

Below: A landmark familiar to all Carlisle citizens is Dixon's chimney erected in 1835 to tower above its factory. All towns have such a landmark whether intended or not. This chimney does give a sense of the industrial development of Carlisle which seemed to be concentrated in the South and South West areas following the line of the River Caldew like the expanding railway line. The textile industries like Dixons which began contemporary industrial development found the water of the river of such excellent quality. This view of Kendal Street looking towards Shaddongate was taken in the 1940s and shows the coping at the top of the chimney resembling, some say, a top hat. However this was removed some 10 years later as it was considered dangerous. The name of the street was given to it by the founder of Carr's Biscuit Works, Jonathan Carr who was born in Kendal and so named the street after his home town. Streets of terraced housing like Kendal Street were soon to be built to accommodate the factory's workers. Streets such as Richard Street, Milbourne Street, Brewery Row all followed similar patterns before slum clearance in the 1930s relieved the area of what would be, if nothing else, a hazard to health.

Right: A commemorative box made by the Metal box company shows the Queen on horseback. These kind of boxes were a great feature of the company's work. One of their most striking was for the troops fighting the Boer War. Queen Victoria gave each soldier a box of chocolates with the box a product of Hudson Scott as the Carlisle firm was known then. This was repeated when the company produced a similar kind of tin box for Queen Mary for the soldiers 'celebrating' the first Christmas of the 1914-18 War. Every coronation of Britain's monarchs and royal marriage was commemorated in this way - an embossed tin made in Carlisle. Hudson Scotts became part of the Metal Box company in the 1920s and efforts to transfer the Carlisle works to London were stoutly resisted, quite properly too for the Hudson Scott company was one of the mainstays of the local economy employing in 1906 over 1200 employees at the James Street factory. When you think of the firms that Metal Box manufactured tins and cans for it is easy to understand the role it played in this industry. Tobacco tins for Players, Talc for Yardleys, Tea for Ringtons, Biscuits for Carrs, naturally, boot polish, toffee, beer and so many more. There was a social aspect to it for the employees with for example a Metal Box cricket team at one time playing in the Cumberland Senior League. In the 1950s the company made 80 percent of the tins manufactured in this country, Carlisle and Metal Box have moved forward. The old hand-made process of 100 cans per hour in 1938 became when automation moved in 900 per minute. Expansion meant a new plant at Botcherby but James Street, referred to by the original company name, was the one associated most deeply with it.

The worst thing about doing handstands at home is sometimes you fall over and sometimes when you fall over and your name is Frances Templeton, you hurt yourself so badly you cry and mam and dad take you to the Cumberland Infirmary. It is not very far from your house but you don't like being hurt. The doctors tell your mam and dad you have to stay there for one whole week until you get better but mam and dad can visit you every day. There is not much to do there, though there are lots of other poorly children to play with and you do have a play table. The nurse has her own desk and when some of the other children are too noisy or a bit naughty or won't take their medicine, the nurse tells us all off. The doctor comes to see you and we hide behind the green screen and when he has finished, the nurse folds it back. Sometime you can play in the toy car but you can't go fast or you might hurt someone then it is put away behind that kind of a cupboard with a sink in. You will be glad when you get home to play with your sister and you won't play handstands again until your dad shows you how to do it properly.

Left: The removal of the tramlines from St Nicholas Street in 1967 must have been one of the last links with the old system of tramways in the city. The first public passenger tram came into service on 30th June 1900, the only event of note on that supposedly historic day was the old lady who boarded the tram and promptly refused to pay as she insisted she had read in the paper the trams were for the benefit of the people. For the next few years the people of Carlisle enjoyed the luxury of the trams until the corporation like many other authorities began to examine the possibilities of a motor omnibus service. So on 21st November 1931 the tram cars were filled with passengers for the last time. The cars on their way to the depot were cheered by people who had come to say farewell to a familiar sight on the roads of the city. Some put railway fog signals on the lines and at the London Road depot several hundred waited for the last car to arrive. It was driven into the depot and, to the urging of the passengers, was driven out again to the strains of 'Auld Lang Syne'. The very last car to Newton was driven by George Scaife and the conductor Mr Hamilton, handed over to the longest serving member of staff, Joe Foster. He was presented with the controller handle as a memento, and 30 years of tramway in Carlisle was ended. However on the following Monday, a driver was in court, his crime was being drunk in charge of a tram at 10.30pm on the last

night. It appeared people had been too kind to him on that last night's final journey and gave him too much to drink. The court was rather lenient with him and, as he was losing his job anyway, his name was not publicly disclosed.

Above: These are the first official post-war ambulances of the Carlisle Ambulance Service. The photograph was taken in 1948 shortly after the two men joined the service after serving in the Army. On the right is Bob Richardson with one big Austin. On the left standing proudly with the Morris is Jim Templeton. These were the only two ambulances at the time for the whole of the city and six men only covered this massive area. When you think of the sophisticated vehicles and the equipment that modern ambulances are today and compare them with these, you wonder how these men could cope. But cope they did and they had to. The country was just recovering from the war and local authorities had to rebuild the structure of service in every area for which they had responsibility. It took time and the acquisition of two new ambulances was then a step forward as the city tried to provide a service to its citizens which they deserved and which could be afforded. The economy of the country and therefore the local one too had yet to grow and the nation had to wait until we had a health service and local emergency services worthy of the name 'service'.

Below: Two stalwarts of the Carlisle Police Force, PCs Richard Cowan, better known as Dick, and Shaw Millican, on the right, pose with their Austin Cambridge Patrol car in the police and fire station yard on Warwick Street. In the 1950s traffic policemen did not drive around in highly luminous, high speed cars; they had saloon cars to do their job. Both men had joined the force after the second world war and were highly respected policeman, described as firm but fair. They served in the days when the police were given the public respect they deserved. Shaw Millican, apart from being a traffic policeman, could always be found on Warwick Road outside Brunton Park on match days giving to anyone whom he thought needed them the encouraging words of 'Move on or I'll move you in'. Dick Cowan later became a well respected Inspector before retiring a few years ago, not to put his feet up but, among other things, to become a staunch and very active member of the Veteran's Choir which gives regular concerts and shows for charity or just purely to entertain. Both men are well remembered as good, effective policemen and certainly as 'characters' and that is a tribute which any police officer would like to have said about him.

Right: A friendly professional chat takes place between Police Sergeant Ronnie Rutherford and Constable Roger Milburn on the cobbled street where Annetwell Street meets Abbey Street outside the Irish Gate Tavern at the western end of the city. The three city gates, Irish, Scotch and English were the three main city gates and were at one time locked at night either to keep people in or out. The gist of the conversation between the men is not revealed but no doubt it would be in the best traditions of the force. These were the days of the Carlisle city police, a small force compared to those of other cities. One advantage of it being a local force was that it did create a bond with the city and between the men which probably larger forces cannot do. It remained as a city force until local government reorganisation in the 1970s. The Tavern for some reason was known as the Blazing Barrel. It is funny how pubs often with the most memorable or historic name often acquire a nickname which only the locals can explain. One in another nearby town was always referred to as the Vatican although it was officially the Sailor's Return. To the right of the Tavern were the married quarters of the Border Regiment although they were termed 'accommodation' they were reputed to be not very accommodating.

Chief Fire Officer Frank Lorrigan looks on as the members of the Carlisle Fire Service and the Auxiliary Fire Service carry out an exercise on Eden Bridge in the 1950s with the old Green Goddess fire engines. Listening to this chief's instructions in the middle of the pavement is Leading Fireman Haggie. It all seems very casual as the other firemen stand on the bridge watching their colleagues below but the interest of the passers by with their dogs has not been maintained. And where are the owners of the two bicycles? What is interesting about the Eden Bridge was that the remains of an old medieval bridge were found when the site was cleared in 1961 for the new Civic Centre, while under the existing one were found the remains of a Roman crossing. Therefore the crossing of the Eden was not always in this position and there is evidence of maybe eight crossing points in this vicinity. Whether the firemen on this exercise are aware of this is another matter. More than likely they will be more concerned about whether they get it right for the chief.

Celebrating a hundred successful years in business

WB Anderson and Sons Ltd is well-known today as a successful property company; having been in this business since the mid 1970s, and it might come as quite a surprise to many people to learn that roots from which this company has grown were planted in the wholesale fruit and vegetable business more than a hundred years ago by William Blaycock Anderson.

Towards the end of the last century William Anderson and his brother John set up as a wholesale fruit and vegetable business in Carlisle. Before long William took the business over, backed by the then substantial sum of £50 which his father had given to him.
This was in 1898, and William Blaycock Anderson was still in his teens. Young W B Anderson turned out to be an excellent businessman; the business prospered, opening a second branch at Workington in 1912 and a third at Whitehaven in 1915, followed by another six branches between 1921 and 1925. The company also began importing produce from overseas, and an office was opened in Liverpool in 1924 to handle imports. In 1926 the business became a Private Limited Company. Over the next 30 years expansion continued in Northern England and Southern Scotland.

From the wholesale depots the company was able to provide a very comprehensive, regular and

Above: The founder of the company, Mr WB Anderson.
Below: The bananas were carried by specially insulated steam heated vans.

efficient sales service across the border counties. A large fleet of motor vehicles had by now taken over from the horses and carts which had provided William Blaycock's first means of transport, and regular deliveries of all kinds of fruit and vegetables were made to the shops; the company also purchased several long distance transport vehicles which were used to carry home grown produce direct from the growers to all its depots for distribution to shops.

At the same time the Company was building up its imports; the importing side of the business became a completely separate department, run mainly from the Liverpool and Glasgow offices and, later, an office in London's Spitalfields Market. William Blaycock attached great importance to establishing personal contact with the people with whom he had dealings, and both he and his two sons John and William, who joined the business in 1937, having previously worked for Fyffes, travelled abroad to meet the growers and to learn first-hand about the produce they were handling. W B Anderson was one of the largest handlers of bananas from the time of their introduction into the country; the bananas were shipped green and ripened in their own banana rooms.

The year 1937 brought an invitation from the Knutsen Shipping Line of Norway for

Above: W B Andersons' fruit and potato cart.
Left: A picture dating from the mid 1970s. It shows Jimmy Robinson, Transport Manger on the left with Ian Ditchburn, coach painter and sign writer. The vehicle was used for the sale and distribution of fruit and vegetables.

William Blaycock Anderson to go on a trip with them to the west coast of America. William Blaycock himself was not able to absent himself from the business at that time, but it was arranged that his sons would go in his place, and John and William spent five months in California, Oregon, Washington State, British Columbia and Virginia, where they learnt a great deal about picking and packing fruit.

The business suffered something of a hiccup during the war, especially the import section which was temporarily closed down.

During the war years the company also became involved in the distribution of cooking oils and fats. Even when wartime restrictions were lifted, local committees, set up by the post-war government, dictated trading conditions. However, business gradually returned to normal, links with overseas suppliers were re-established and new contacts were made.

When William Blaycock died in 1949, his sons John and William took over the business. November 20th 1958 was the 60th anniversary of the end of William Blaycock Anderson's first year's trading on his own account, and although sadly he did not live to to see the occasion, John and William, the Joint Managing Directors, marked the firm's Diamond Jubilee by awarding every employee £1 for every completed year of service with the Company, as a token of appreciation. The company remained at its original premises in West Walls until the end of the 1950s, when it moved to Durranhill Trading Estate to allow for modernisation and expansion. A change of direction had become necessary because the supermarkets' increasing share of the consumer market was having an impact on the distribution channels and

> W. B. ANDERSON & SONS LIMITED.
>
> DIAMOND JUBILEE, 1898-1958.
>
> On 20th November, 1898, the late Mr. W. B. Anderson completed his first year's trading on his own account, so the Firm celebrates its Diamond Jubilee this month. To mark the occasion the Directors have decided that every employee should receive £1 for every completed year of service with the Company as a token of their appreciation of your loyal service to the Company.
>
> Yours truly,
> JOHN ANDERSON,
> WILLIAM ANDERSON,
> (Joint Managing Directors).

Above: In celebration of the diamond jubilee the directors had decided that every employee should receive £1 for every completed year. Dating back to 1958.
Below: Inside the warehouse in 1959.

built up over its years in business. This included the Head office at Durranhill Trading Estate which has recently seen the complete refurbishment to accommodate Lynx Express Parcels and other tenants.

Since launching out on its new venture, the company has not looked back; it has pursued a policy of investment in quality commercial property and established itself

threatening to undermine the network which WB Anderson had established. Diversification came in the form of vegetable growing, pre-packing, haulage and export of seed potatoes.

The third generation of Andersons joined the family business, Jonathan in the late 60s and Philip in 1972.

In 1976 a decision was made to sell the fruit and vegetable business, excluding the properties, to West Cumberland Farmers. This left the company with both capital to invest and a substantial portfolio of commercial property which it had

in the property market. The company will continue to build upon its success in this field in the future, but as a family firm it has not lost sight of the tradition upon which it was founded, and still remembers its founder, William Blaycock Anderson, with the greatest respect. Celebrating a hundred successful years in business.

Above: This picture dates back to November 1955, when John Anderson visited Sacramento, the headquarters of the California Fruit Exchange.
Below: The company site at Stevenson Road, Durranhill in 1959.

Stead McAlpin - Cummersdale Print Works

Calico printing began in Carlisle in the 1760s and quickly became established as the principal local industry, providing employment for over a thousand people by the end of the century. One of the many printworks operating in the area during the first part of the 19th century was the Stampery Printworks at Wigton, and around 1828 Thomas McAlpin, son of a tenant farmer, was taken into partnership there with Richard Halliley and his son Richard. Church records of the time show Thomas and his brothers John, Duncan and William as calico printers, and it is presumed that they learned the trade and spent most of their working lives at the Stampery Printworks. However, in 1835 Thomas resigned from there and leased a disused textile printing mill at Cummersdale, subsequently purchasing the site when an opportunity arose in 1844. Standing next to the River Caldew, which provided the water needed both in the various processes and to power the machinery, this printworks had been built in 1801 and had stood unoccupied since 1817. Thomas had repairs and renovations carried out, and installed a four coloured copper cylinder printing machine, for which he paid £200. He was joined in the venture by Duncan, John's son Hugh, and Thomas's stepson John Stead; Thomas had married a widow, Mrs Mary Stead, in 1827 after the death of his first wife a decade before, and the business connection with the Stead family was to continue until the retirement of John Stead's great grandson R G Diggle in 1980.

Within a year of commencing production, Thomas and Hugh McAlpin, Stead and Company was trading throughout England, Scotland and Ireland. It produced mainly furnishing chintzes printed on calicos, and also printed onto mousseline de laine, a fine wool fabric used for dresses and shawls. The company originally used both the modern engraved copper roller printing process and the traditional wooden hand blocks. This latter technique involved cutting away the surface of the block to leave the design in relief; copper wire or nails could be added for fine detail, or felt pads could be inserted for strong definition. Separate blocks were cut for each colour and for each section of a design. Dye was then applied to the block and it was pressed onto the prepared fabric; the design was built up by the successive application of each block. Hand block printing produced superior results, but was a time-consuming and therefore expensive process; for instance, the Tree of Life, a complex design by textile designer Harry Wearne in the early 20th century, required 390 blocks and had a repeat of 8' 6". It took two years to cut the blocks, and the fabric was then printed at a rate of 12 yards in 12 hours. McAlpin, Stead and Company continued using this traditional method for much longer than most companies, alongside modern techniques such as surface roller printing using wooden rollers which was introduced 1844. When the Wigton Stampery was declared bankrupt in 1847, some of the equipment, including printing blocks, was purchased for the Cummersdale works. In 1871 copper printing machines for up to 10 colours were purchased, and some handblocks were destroyed at this time in anticipation of the end of hand processes, although in fact hand block printing was not completely phased out until 1977. Many of the designs were transferred from the blocks onto screens, and are still printed today.

The company recorded some noteworthy successes in the mid 1800s; they were awarded a silver medal at the Exhibition of the Society of Arts in London in 1849, received a favourable mention at the Great Exhibition of 1851 where they had entered their fabrics, and won another medal at the International Furniture Exhibition in 1862. A floral chintz printed by McAlpin Stead was chosen by Queen Victoria for the royal yacht, and this has been known as the Victoria and Albert chintz ever since.

Above: One of the certificates of child labour which was common practice in the 1870s.

Textile printing was a very skilled trade and involved serving a long apprenticeship. The trade was often passed down from father to son, and working at Cummersdale became a tradition in a lot of families, making Stead, McAlpin and Company very much a family firm where many apprentices already had a relative working there. There was also work for women, and youngsters aged eight and upwards were employed as messengers, copper roller pattern painters and tierers. The tierer's main job was to brush colour onto a sieve cloth, a thick piece of felt floating on a sieve, onto which the printer then laid his block to cover it with colour. By law, juvenile employees had to spend part of their working day receiving schooling, and in 1846 a schoolmistress was employed by the company and a school was opened at the works.

During the late 1840s and early 1850s the management of the company devolved to the younger generation following the death of Thomas and the retirement of Duncan; Hugh McAlpin and John Stead were joined by Nathan Stead McAlpin, but Hugh died in 1858, and in 1867 Nathan retired, leaving John Stead in sole charge. By this time the company was employing some 250 people, and was the only textile printing mill surviving in Cumberland.

John Stead continued to invest in further equipment, including multi-coloured copper roller printing machinery, and he also developed his own machine to print on both sides window blind fabric, taking out a patent in 1880. In 1892 John Stead died, and

Above: Notice the women tierers in this photograph taken during the first world war when there was a shortage of male workers. The tierers above were the printer's assistants; they had to supply him with colour.
Below: A later example of women hand screen printing.

his son Edmund Wright Stead took over; the following year Stead McAlpin acquired the blocks, machinery and 9,000 designs from Bannister Hall, a long-established textile printworks near Preston, Lancashire, and one of Stead McAlpin's major competitors in the field of high quality hand blocked fabrics. This acquisition put Stead McAlpin in an even stronger position. Expansion continued with the purchase of neighbouring buildings: a cotton mill which was used to house the block printing department and to provide storage room for the thousands of hand blocks; a corn mill which was used for storage for a time and then leased out; and the dyeing and bleaching works of James Mungal, which was leased to a group of local businessmen who ran it until 1911, after which it was used as extra storage space for Stead McAlpin.

In 1924 the limited company of Stead, McAlpin and Company was formed; Edmund Wright Stead was Governing Director until his death ten years later, during which period the major technological advance was the introduction of hand screen printing. A series of trials was held, and when the process had proved successful a building was erected to house the 70-yard tables; however, it was not until after the second world war that full use was made of this method.

Various celebrations marked the works centenary in 1935. One of the events organised was a sports day with an entertaining range of competitions including a tug-of-war won by the Engravers, and a veteran's race in which the oldest competitor, 70 year old Mr Beaty, came second. In the same year the company exhibited at the British

Top: Part of the "bottom village", with the block factory (old cotton mill).
Above: This sample is taken from an apprentice's work book in 1905.

Industries Fair at London's White City.
During the second world war textile printing was designated a non-essential industry, and war work, such as sorting rivets, bolts and washers and repairing aircraft fuel tanks, was carried out in the works. Hand block printing for export was allowed to continue, and a few items such as scarves with regimental insignia and patriotic slogans were produced for the home market to boost morale. Printing blocks were heavy and block printing had previously been strictly a job for the men, but it now had to done by women as a result of conscription of the male workforce, which apparently caused much consternation at the time. After the war, the screen printing process was developed, and this was a job for women. The hand screen printing system was later improved by the invention of a glider mechanism which allowed the frame to be slid along the table instead of lifted, making operation easier, and in 1961 automatic flat screen printing machines made the process easier still and much faster.

In 1965 the John Lewis Partnership acquired complete control of the business. The company continued as commission printers, and by 1968 had been officially integrated into the Group. Technology continued to advance; copper roller and surface roller printing ended in 1970, and the following year rotary screen printing was introduced, bringing a number of advantages over flat screen printing. In 1982 the company began to produce plain dyed fabrics, and also, around this time, began to develop its own computer system. More major developments came in 1984 with the installation of a new

continuous bleach range in the Cloth Preparation Department, with automatic sensors and touch-button control; and in the same year there were important advances in the colour making and dye systems.

Further innovations at Stead McAlpin continued with a sophisticated Stead McAlpin Colour Graphics System, and it is this constant pursuit of development through innovation which has kept the company at the head of the industry. With production now centred on upholstery and curtain fabric, it offers short run, multi-colour printing on a wide range of cotton, linen, viscose and polyester cloths using its excellent design separation and colouring facilities. The end product is destined for the main furnishing fabric houses at the top end of the market, both at home and for export customers, notably America. These fabrics are often featured in the glossy home furnishing magazines. A complete service is provided to customers, from cloth procurement, bleaching, dyeing, printing and warehousing; in 1990 a new warehouse was opened on site to house not only Stead's finished stocks but all the John Lewis Partnership fabrics.

Stead McAlpin is a modern, forward-looking company, focused on customer service, competitiveness, productivity and profitability. However, its success lies in its unique combination of traditional skills and innovative thinking; it is a company which is proud of its long history and tradition. One hundred and fifty years of achievements were commemorated at its Sesquicentenary Exhibition at the Tullie House Museum, Carlisle, in 1985; and the company's extensive archive is in itself a fascinating historical record. With its earliest piece dating back to 1789, this archive of over 25,000 designs contains many prized works, including some William Morris designs acquired in 1940. An invaluable legacy of the past, this collection will continue to be a source of inspiration to designers for many years to come.

Left: A close view of a printer and a tierer.

This firm accounts for the success of its clients

James Watson Senior, founder of one of the accountancy firms which later joined to form Armstrong Watson, began his career in a city with a population of barely 29,000, where there was no telephone and no electricity and the only connections with the outside world were the Newcastle railway line, the canal to Port Carlisle, or the stage coach in the late 19th century. James Watson's first appointment was in the accounting office at Messrs Peter Dixon and Sons, cotton spinners and weavers, at Warwick Bridge, and he subsequently transferred to the Shaddongate Works where he was in charge of the accounting office. His next move took him to Wigan, to the colliery of Messrs Rylands and Co, but this appointment was short-lived because, as his obituary tells us, 'the air in that town did not suit Mrs Watson's health'. He returned to the more therapeutic air of Carlisle with his wife and young son, James Watson Junior who had been born in 1868, and set up his own practice at Old Post Office Court.

The Institute of Chartered Accountants was established in 1880, and it was 1877 when James Watson began his practice. Up until the granting of the Royal Charter, accountancy was not the well-respected profession which it has since

Above: Partners and staff of James Watson & Son.
Below: The market place, Brampton. In 1935, an office was opened in Brampton and this picture was taken at the time of the Coronation of King George V.

become; in most people's minds, accountants were associated with insolvency, so businesses tried to have as little to do with accountants as possible. James Watson was one of the earliest representatives of the newly-established profession in the Carlisle area. On one occasion at least he may have found his chosen career more exciting than he bargained for; a report in the Carlisle Journal and Carlisle Patriot tells how, at a local Annual Meeting, 'Mr G (the Secretary) came in drunk and Mr Watson pointed out that an error had been made, asking him kindly to alter it. Mr G said, "I will not." Mr Watson said, "Please yourself, Mr G. Here is a four and it should be a six, making a difference of 200." Mr G said that he was master in that place and Mr Watson was simply an auditor. Mr G then produced a knife and said, "You are a sneak. You are a cheat . . . you are, Mr Watson, and you want my place."' And in the ensuing struggle Mr Watson was obliged to 'fell' Mr G twice in order to avoid personal injury. However, clients such as 'Mr G' must have been in a minority as James Watson Senior still considered accountancy a fit profession for his son. James Watson Junior duly served articles with John Jackson Saint at 10 Bank Street, was admitted in 1890 and was taken into partnership with his father, practising from Devonshire Buildings at 24 Devonshire Street, later known as Lloyds Bank Chambers.

James Watson Senior died in 1911, aged 75, and his son continued running the firm, guiding it through the war and then through the depression of the 20s and 30s. From what has been recorded of those days, James Watson Junior seems to have enjoyed a very orderly lifestyle; each morning his private chauffeur drove him to Lowther Street, where he visited a barber for his morning shave before crossing the street to his offices and beginning the day's work by opening the mail himself. On Thursday afternoon, he generally caught the train to Silloth to play a round of golf. He never married, but continued to live with his sister at the family home in St James Road until his death in 1941.

The partners of the firm at the time of James Watson Junior's death were Ernest William Glaister and Jonathan Sharp. Ernest Glaister had been articled to James Watson Junior and was admitted into partnership shortly after the death of James Watson Senior in 1911, and Johnston Sharp was admitted as a partner in 1939. The latter had been a senior employee for 25 years,

Top left: Thomas Dowell, partner from 1943 - 1957.
Top centre: John Mungo Glaister, partner from 1911 -1953. Top right: Ernest William Glaister, partner from 1911 - 1953
Above: The preface of the company's historical handbook.

firm built up a comprehensive knowledge of farm accounts, and farmers have remained an important category of client to this day.

The late 50s saw the death of Thomas Dowell and John Mungo Glaister, both at the age of 63. Both had been very popular members of the community; John was sadly missed by his farming clients

having joined the firm in 1909, aged 19, after serving three years as a sea-going engineer with the Wallsend Slipway Company. The partners were joined in 1943 by Thomas Dowell and John Mungo Glaister, and after Ernest Glaister's retirement in 1953 Kenneth Johnston Sharp, son of Johnston Sharp, was also admitted as a Partner; Kenneth had graduated with Honours from St John's College, Cambridge after serving with the Indian Army between 1945 and 1948. He was to become the youngest President of the Institute of Chartered Accountants, holding this position from 1973-4, and later receiving a Knighthood for his services as Head of the Government Accountancy Services.

During the 1940s the firm found its services increasingly in demand amongst a new sector of the community, whose appreciation of the good advice they received took the form of rabbits, fresh eggs and other such items, which were especially welcome in wartime. The clients were, of course, farmers, and it was initially John Mungo Glaister who took a special interest in their affairs. Over the years the

Above: Luncheon at Moorgate Place, London to celebrate Mr Johnson Sharp's 74th year as member of the Institute of Chartered Accountants in May 1988.
Right: Annual conference in 1983.

who had held him in such high regard, while the local music and dramatic circles were greatly saddened by the loss of Thomas, who had taken many lead parts in Gilbert and Sullivan productions of the Carlisle Choral Society. After their deaths, the partners were Kenneth Sharp and Robert Douglas Thomlinson who had been admitted in 1956, and in 1959 Geoffrey Douglas Shepherd was also admitted to the Partnership.

James Watson and Son was Carlisle's first Chartered Accountants, but another firm of Chartered Accountants had been practising in Carlisle for almost as long. This was Armstrong Routledge and Co, which existed between 1906 and 1921 as Greaves and Armstrong. When that partnership was dissolved, Herbert Joseph Armstrong continued in practice under the name of H J Armstrong and Co from 57 English Street, Carlisle, and also from his native Newcastle upon

Tyne where he had premises in Emerson Chambers, Blackett Street. William Wake Routledge joined the firm as an articled clerk in 1919, qualified in 1924 and was admitted as a Partner in 1926. From 1927, William effectively ran the Carlisle offices and Herbert Armstrong practised in Newcastle until his retirement in 1940. In that same year John Mark Fendley joined the firm as an articled clerk; his articles were interrupted by the war, when he was posted on active service in France and Germany. He qualified in 1950 and was introduced as a partner in 1953.

In 1960 the firms of Armstrong Routledge and Co and James Watson and Son 'entered into a mutual arrangement . . . whereby the Partners in each of our respective firms become Partners in the other'. From this time on, expansion has been been steady. Initially each firm continued to operate from its own premises; an association with the Penrith firm of Milburn and Dawson led to the formation of Armstrong Watson and Milburn in 1964, and in 1965 a further association with R L Wyllie and Co of Whitehaven resulted in the name expanding to

Armstrong Watson Milburn Wyllie and Co. Since that time a number of partners have been admitted, sometimes in consequence of a series of acquisitions made by the firm, and new branches have been opened, including those at Keswick, Dumfries, Annan and Leeds. Two subsidiaries, Cumbria Computer Services Ltd and A W Investments Limited, were formed, in 1974 and 1972 respectively. The firm's Carlisle offices moved to the current premises in Victoria Place in April 1967, and the name Armstrong Watson and Co was adopted in 1971.

Today, Armstrong Watson and Co provides financial advice to a wide range of business and personal clients. Backed by more than a century's experience and by continuous investment in staff training, the firm remains committed to the pursuit of excellence, and recognises that the success of its clients is the best measure of its own success. Sir Walter Scott once wrote, 'On the Borders were the Armstrongs, able men, somewhat unruly, and very ill to tame'. Over the years the unruly, untameable tendencies which Sir Walter Scott thought he detected may have mellowed, but the ability which he observed has remained a characterstic of this firm throughout. It is the exceptional ability of all its staff which has earned the enduring respect and loyalty of clients and brought Armstrong Watson and Co to the very forefront of its profession.

Above: Fairview House, Armstrong Watson & Co's corporate office in Victoria Place, Carlisle.
Below: Armstrong Watson & Co. The company partners in November 1998.

Keeping Carlisle well furnished

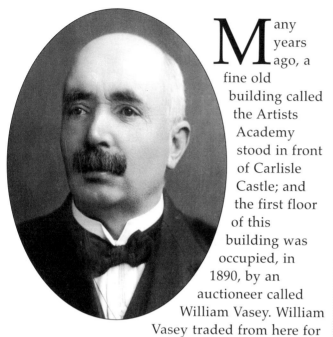

Many years ago, a fine old building called the Artists Academy stood in front of Carlisle Castle; and the first floor of this building was occupied, in 1890, by an auctioneer called William Vasey. William Vasey traded from here for a number of years; his three sons, Harold, Arthur and John Kay, joined him in the business, and Anne, one of his five daughters, helped out at the auctions as a bookkeeper before she married. Arthur subsequently left to set his son William up in purpose-built garage premises, at the end of East Tower Street, but the other two sons stayed; Harold, a lifelong bachelor, took charge of the furniture side of the business, while John was the auctioneer, and they were joined by Anne's husband, Jack Porter.

After trading at the Academy for several years, the firm moved to new premises at the top end of Fisher Street, behind Bulloughs. It was while they were here that W Vasey and Sons began dealing in new furniture, and because of the layout of the shop this involved them in a lot of lifting work. The collection of second-hand furniture was an on-going process throughout the week, and selling was a once-a-week event. Meanwhile, the new furniture was on display on the shop floor; but on sale day all the space on the shop floor was needed for the buyers to assemble. So the new furniture had be piled up in the window to make room for the buyers, and at the end of the day when they had gone it was brought back out of the window and put on display again. This was far from an ideal arrangement! However, a few years later the firm moved again, to 50-52 Scotch Street, where they had a long narrow shop with a high ceiling and a separate auction room to the rear; so the weekly ritual of shifting the new furniture in and out of the window was no longer necessary.

In 1935 W Vasey and Sons opened its first branch, in Great Dockray, Penrith. This branch was run by the two Jimmys; Jimmy Ismay, the husband of Jean, another of William Vasey's daughters, was the manager, and Jimmy Ellwood was his trusted assistant. People today still remember both Jimmys with great affection. Jimmy Ismay died prematurely; he was a loveable person, and was sadly missed by many people. Jimmy Ellwood took over as Manager, and ran the store for many years. Customers may know that he died recently, after a short retirement.

Shortly after the opening of the Penrith branch, war broke out. This was a trying time for the business. In order to sell second-hand furniture it was necessary to hold a licence, and this had to be renewed every week. Furniture was subject to price control, and often sales were decided by drawing names out of a hat. The range of new furniture available was also severely restricted; it was all utility furniture, with a choice of two designs for the upholstery and two bedroom

Above: W Vasey the founder of the company.
Below: W Vasey as a young soldier.

Left: The Central Hall where W Vasey began trading.

studying, and eventually he could bear it no longer. When he had almost reached the stage of sitting his finals, he abandoned his studies and ran away to Edinburgh, where he enrolled in the Navy and was posted to Burma to help set up signal stations. In due course he returned, with the intention of completing his studies, but his father persuaded him to join the family firm instead, as Harold and Jack's health restricted their activities and there was no-one else to take over the new furniture side of the business.

A few years after the end of the war, W Vasey and Sons took over Whittles in Whitehaven. As the business began to prosper again, their Scotch Street

designs, all, again, subject to strict price control. However, W Vasey and Sons rose to the challenge and managed to stay in business, but by the end of the war both Harold and his brother-in-law Jack Porter were suffering from ill health. Arthur's son William was called up, and as a result of this he lost his garage business, but on his return from the war he took over the old established firm of Donaldson. Meanwhile his cousin Malcolm, the son of John Kay, decided to train as a surveyor and was articled to John Wright, of Jos M Richardson and Son of Cecil Street. Being an adventurous young man, he found it difficult to watch all his older friends being called up while he stayed at home

premises began to grow, first upwards with the addition of an extra floor, then outwards with the aquisition of adjoining properties as they became available. The company then purchased a state managed public house called The Blue Bell, an old coaching house with a fine minstrel gallery. This was subsequently developed into the adjoining building, but because it was a listed building the original facade was preserved.

The end of 1972 and beginning of 1973 was a sad time for the business. Derek Ismay, Jimmy Ismay's son, had trained as an auctioneer to assist and eventually take over from John Kay, but sadly Derek died very young, and a few months

later John Kay also died. This left the firm without an auctioneer, and the loss of both men was a great blow to the community as well as to the business. Derek, with his quiet and courteous ways, had been well liked by the customers. John Kay was a respected member of the community, having stood as an Independant candidate in Denton Holme ward for several years. He was never afraid to speak his mind, and was well known for his outspoken views on issues which he believed in.

The deaths of John Kay and Derek left Malcolm in charge of the company on his own, and it was simply not possible for one man to run both the auction-eering and the furniture aspects of the business. Although he was very reluctant to give up auctioneering after more than 90 years, this ultimately proved to be the only possible course of action. Shortly after this, Jack Porter's son came into the business for a while, but left to pursue his interest in Council affairs, successfully standing as Council member for a number of years. The current proprietor of the business, Malcolm's son Michael Vasey, then joined his father and took over the furniture buying.

Left: An early interior view of the Scotch Street premises.
Below: Whittle's store in Whitehaven.

over the years by trading on service and quality, and by not offering any gimmicks. Customer satisfaction is of paramount importance, and if complaints do arise the company always does its best to put matters right. The proprietors also wish to acknowledge the valued help of their loyal staff, past and present, many of whom have now retired and can look back on a long and happy employment with this well-established and very professional family firm.

The decision to move from Scotch Street to Lancaster Street came about relatively suddenly, and was influenced by a combination of factors. One factor was the Council's plan to pedestrianise Scotch Street, which would have made it difficult to load and unload furniture. A second factor was that a prospective purchaser came forward with an offer for the Scotch Street premises, and the third factor was that a site on Lancaster Street came onto the market. Unlike Scotch Street, this site had ample parking space, making it ideal for the furniture trade. The move therefore went ahead, and the Lancaster Street premises are today one of W Vasey and Son's two trading outlets in Carlisle. The firm has in recent years diversified into more modern furniture. Michael decided that it would be better to display modern styles separately from traditional designs, and Galeria on Currock Road was bought for this purpose. The most modern lines can now be seen at Galeria, while at Lancaster Street customers can choose from an extensive range of traditional furniture.

W Vasey and Sons has built up the goodwill of its customers

Top left: The Scotch Street store pictured in 1988.
Below: The carpet showroom of the Scotch Street Store.
Bottom: The modern spacious showroom of the newest premises on Lancaster Street.

In all things Charity

Austin Friars School, St Ann's Hill, Carlisle, combines the best traditions of a Catholic School with the academic and sporting achievements that complement modern life. Thus boys and girls educated here gain a solid education founded on enduring Christian precepts together with experience of the world in which they will make their way.

The tall sandstone building, shaped like a letter T was built as a convent in 1892. Between then and 1903, when the nuns moved to Newcastle, girls were taught at St Ann's Hill . In the late 1940s the owners, The Poor Sisters of Nazareth, who wished to dispose of the property, were pleased to find a buyer who would use the magnificent chapel daily.

Father Colman O'Driscoll, founder of Austin Friars School, dedicated the school to the service of God on the 4th July 1951. For the first time since Henry VIII's Dissolution of the Monasteries in 1540 the Augustinian Friars were once again part of the educational scene in England. Initially the austere building, no longer known as Nazareth House, housed the entire school of 78 boys with space to spare. This was known to be a temporary arrangement as the governors and staff had faith that their school would soon outgrow a single building.

Within five years the Preparatory Department for the under thirteens was transferred to Ellingham Hall at Chathill in Northumberland. The space vacated in the former convent for seniors was insufficient to meet the demand from families requiring a sound education. Building work in the late 1950s provided new dormitories in the attics, formerly used for recreational purposes, plus new classrooms in the spacious basement of the large Victorian building. This expansion programme was generously funded by contributions from the English houses of the Augustinian Order.

Above: The first members of staff at Austin Friars School. Below: The very first photograph of pupils at Austin Friars in 1953.

The school motto 'In omnibus caritas' ('In all things charity'), reflects the caring spirit of St Augustine, and the school's Chaplaincy Team cares for the spiritual and pastoral needs of pupils and staff and, on occasion, parents.

The well tried 'house' system was adopted by the school from its early days to give youngsters a sense of belonging to, and pride in, their smaller part of the greater community. The house names, Clare, Lincoln and Stafford were chosen for their pre-Reformation Augustinian links.

Regular Parents' Evenings at which staff and parents meet ease full co-operation between home and school. The staff at Austin Friars liaises closely with pupils' parents to monitor the children's academic progress; in the Fourth and Fifth Forms emphasis is on pupils choosing subjects which will offer them a wide choice of career. English Language and Literature, Maths, RE and Physical Education are, of course, compulsory subjects, and Additional Mathematics lessons are given to Fifth Form students who pass their Maths GCSE a year early. The Library Resources Centre is fully computerised and equipped with CD-ROMs,

videos and audio tapes. With an eye to the children's future the school has a clear emphasis on science and technology, computer literacy and keyboard skills, and two members of staff are devoted to careers guidance. Sixth Form students are given real business experience across a full academic year with an eye to developing skills in leadership, team work, responsibility, financial and quality control, making presentations, producing company reports and management.

Recent GCSE results underline Austin Friars' success, revealing that an amazing 90.4 percent of pupils achieve five or more passes at levels A*, A, B or C. 'A' level results show an overall pass rate of 89 percent, and most Sixth Formers go on to enter university.

Top left: Altar servers in the School Chapel in 1955. Top right: Chris McGeorge who attended Austin Friars School in 1974 - 81, this photograph was taken at the Brisbane Commonwealth Games in 1982. Left: School Sports have an important role to play.

Academic achievement goes hand in hand with both outdoor education and the community activities which together develop the unique personality of each individual. An extensive programme of sports flourishes in the school, with rugby and hockey taking first place during the autumn and spring terms, and cricket, athletics and tennis are taught as part of the programme in the summer. Netball, basketball, volleyball, cross country and swimming are only a few of the alternative sports offered by the school, whose dedication was recognised by the prestigious Sportsmark Award of the English Sports Council.

Austin Friars can be justifiably proud of their sporting achievements; from the time the school won its first athletics shield in the City Sports in 1956 there has been no looking back. The following year the rugby team romped to victory against Carlisle Grammar School for the first time. 'Old boy' Chris McGeorge reflected glory on his former school when he represented England at the 1982 Commonwealth Games in Brisbane, coming third in the 800 metres.

With the continuing good health of the children in mind, the house dining rooms offer a healthy and varied choice of food complementing the fresh air and exercise offered by the extensive games facilities.

Extra-curricular pastimes have always been a vital part of the school, and the staff have found that young

people cement friendships based on shared interests and challenges. The Duke of Edinburgh's Award Scheme and the Outdoor Pursuits expeditions, both at home and abroad, are open to all. The Debating Society teaches youngsters the art of arguing their case in a civilised manner - a useful skill for the leaders of the future.

Speech, Drama and the Performing Arts develop the children's confidence and self-assurance, and singing, both in choirs and solo, is a regular and satisfying part of school life. Austin Friars' groups and individuals participate annually and creditably in the Carlisle Festival. Drawing, painting and photography are complemented by three dimensional work with textiles and more solid materials.

The end product of such a wealth of caring education is a school leaver who is confident in him- or herself and possesses the ability to plan for the future, whatever that may be.

Father Bernard O'Connor, who was headmaster between 1966 and 1973, summed up his own feelings about Austin Friars School in a pertinent statement: 'It was good to be in at the beginning. It is good to see how a young idea has flourished and grown to maturity. When I look back, I recall names and I see faces, and I smile.'

He had plenty to smile about.

*Top: An aerial view of Austin Friars School. **Left:** Sixth formers in the 1980s studying electronics.*

Educating Cumbrians for a better future

The history of Carlisle College stretches back as far as 14 December 1824 when the first Mechanics Institute was formed in the city. The aim of the institute was to 'instruct mechanics and artisans in those branches of Science and Art which were applicable to their trade'.

Work on Carlisle Technical College on its present site began in 1950 and was officially opened on 18 February 1954, offering Engineering, Building, Textiles and Pure Science.

By 1959 Commerce, Construction, General and Physical Education and Food were subjects all being offered on the new site.

The college continued to offer technical education, but gradually the areas of specialism moved towards the service industries. By 1992 it was decided to change the name to Carlisle College and the corporate identity which remains today was introduced.

Since then, Carlisle College (still known fondly as 'the tech' by some local people) has continually moved forward, being in the forefront of modern technology and computing. Today it continues to offer the mix of vocational and academic education to over 12,000 students. The methods of study have also changed now to make the college more accessible by more people. Daytime, evenings, Saturdays, distance learning, video-conferencing, courses in village halls or in mobile learning centres are all ways that students can access a range of learning programmes, from introductory level through to post-graduate qualifications.

Carlisle College won the Queen's Anniversary Prizes for Higher and Further Education in 1996, Investors in People in 1997, was appointed as a

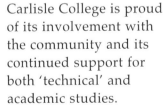

National Centre for Excellence in IT and High Technology in 1998 and was awarded a government Charter Mark for excellence in customer service in 1999.

Carlisle College is proud of its involvement with the community and its continued support for both 'technical' and academic studies.

Top: Lieut. General Sir Ronald Weeks who declared the college open.
Above: The North Elevation of the college in 1954.
Left: The rag charity appeal in April 1959. The college dancing girls with their trainer standing, on the right is Dorothy Harling.

Belah School in a 1950s line up

Acknowledgments

Mr & Mrs Jim Templeton

Alec Alves

Steven White and all the staff of the Local Studies Section of Carlisle Library

Tommy Craig

Margaret Irving

The staff of Carlisle WRVS for allowing us to use material from their archive

Thanks also are due to Kevin McIlroy who penned the editorial captions